Easy
Potluck
Recipes

EASY-TO-MAKE,
EASY-TO-TAKE

Easy Potluck Recipes
Easy-to-Make, Easy-to-Take

1st Printing - May 2006
2nd Printing - May 2007
3rd Printing - February 2009

International Standard Book No. 978-1-931294-81-2 (Paper Cover)

Library of Congress Number: 2006927593 (Paper Cover)

Library of Congress Catalog Data

> Easy potluck recipes : easy-to-make, easy-to-take.
> 157 p. : ill. ; 23 cm.
> Includes index.
> ISBN: 193129481X
> 1. Cookery, American. I. Cookbook Resources, LLC.
> TX715 .E1755 2006
> 641.5973 22

Illustrations by Nancy Murphy Griffith

Edited, Designed, Published and Manufactured in the
United States of America by
Cookbook Resources, LLC
541 Doubletree Drive
Highland Village, Texas 75077
Toll free 866-229-2665

www.cookbookresources.com

cookbook *resources* LLC
Bringing Family and Friends to the Table

• Potluck Pride •

Just when you thought Jello salads, green bean casseroles and supermarket cupcakes were your potluck legacy, *Easy Potluck Recipes* comes to your rescue with mouth-watering dishes for real potluck pride.

Working moms and grandmothers don't have the kitchen time to whip up homemade goodies that take hours of prep and skills of super-moms. *Easy Potluck Recipes* will show you, with very little kitchen time, how you can create eye-popping dishes that change potluck cooking forever.

Learn how to quickly prepare easy delicious, family-sized casseroles for a new couple in town, a church supper, a family reunion, a grieving friend or someone just home from the hospital. These dazzling new dishes will make Aunt Betty think you've been toiling over a hot stove since this time last year.

You can change the ordinary potluck table to one with tasty, exciting new dishes everyone will love. Chuckle as potluckers scurry past all the other dishes to get a piece of your Outrageously Good Chocolate Cookie Cake. Watch helplessly as someone else spoons far more than his share of your delicious looking Neptune's King Crab Casserole. Look happily at the lucky potlucker who is scraping up the last of your Famous Strawberry Salad.

Proudly accept the "Was that your wonderful beef stew?" Congratulations *Easy Potluck Recipes* will show you how to be the pride of your next potluck...Potluck Proud! Soon, all of your fellow potluckers will want to bring tempting dishes like yours to all the potluck dinners. *Easy Potluck Recipes* will assure every potlucker of a palate-pleasing potluck experience.

Contents

Salads Galore

Broccoli-Noodle Crunch Salad

Who thought up the idea of grating broccoli "stems" for a salad? It was pure genius! This salad is different – and very good. It will last and still be "crispy" in the refrigerator for days!

1 cup slivered almonds, toasted	240 ml
1 cup sunflower seeds, toasted	240 ml
2 (3 ounce) packages chicken-flavored ramen noodles	2 (84 g)
1 (12 ounce) package broccoli slaw	340 g

Dressing:

¾ cup oil	180 ml
½ cup white vinegar	120 ml
½ cup sugar	120 ml
Ramen noodles seasoning packet	

• Preheat oven to 275° (135° C). Toast almonds and sunflower seeds in oven for 15 minutes. Break up ramen noodles (but do not cook) and mix with slaw, almonds and sunflower seeds.

• In separate bowl, combine dressing ingredients and noodle seasoning packet. Pour over slaw mixture and mix well. Prepare at least 1 hour before serving.

● ● ●

• • • • • • • • • •

Broccoli Salad

5 cups broccoli florets, stemmed   1.3 L
1 sweet red bell pepper, julienned
1 cup chopped celery   240 ml
8 - 12 ounces Monterey Jack cheese, cubed   227 g

• Combine all ingredients and mix well.

• Toss with Italian or favorite dressing. Refrigerate.

• • •

Green Beans
With Tomatoes

2 pounds frozen, cut green beans   1 kg
4 tomatoes, chopped, drained
1 bunch green onions, chopped
1 cup Italian salad dressing   240 ml

• Place beans in saucepan, cover with water and bring to boil.

• Cook uncovered for 8 to 10 minutes or until tender crisp, drain and chill.

• Add tomatoes, green onions and salad dressing and toss to coat.

• • •

Winter Salad

1 (16 ounce) can French-style green beans, drained	.5 kg
1 (16 ounce) can jalapeno black-eyed peas, drained	.5 kg
1 (16 ounce) can shoe-peg white corn, drained	.5 kg
1 (16 ounce) can English peas, drained	.5 kg
1 (2 ounce) jar chopped pimentos, drained	57 g
1 bell pepper, chopped	
1 onion, sliced, broken into rings	

Dressing:

¾ cup sugar	180 ml
½ teaspoon garlic powder	2 ml
½ cup oil	120 ml
¾ cup vinegar	180 ml

- In 3-quart (3 L) container with lid, combine all salad ingredients plus 2 teaspoons (10 ml) salt and 1 teaspoon (5 ml) pepper and gently mix. Be sure to drain vegetables well before combining.

- To prepare dressing, combine all dressing ingredients and mix well. Pour mixture over vegetables and stir. Cover and chill. Serves 16.

Tip: I keep a supply of these ingredients on hand – and when you need to take a dish to a friend – it's a salad in a hurry.

● ● ●

Marinated Corn Salad

3 (15 ounce) cans whole kernel corn, drained   3 (425 g)
1 red bell pepper, chopped
1 cup chopped walnuts   240 ml
¾ cup chopped celery   180 ml
1 (8 ounce) bottle Italian salad dressing   227 g

• In bowl with lid, combine corn, bell pepper, walnuts
  and celery. (For a special little zip, add several dashes
  hot sauce.)

• Pour salad dressing over vegetables and refrigerate
  several hours before serving.

Mediterranean Potato Salad

2 pounds red-skinned new potatoes, quartered   1 kg
¾ cup Caesar dressing   180 ml
½ cup grated parmesan cheese   120 ml
¼ cup chopped fresh parsley   60 ml
½ cup chopped roasted red peppers   120 ml

• Cook potatoes in boiling water until fork-tender,
  drain and place in large bowl.

• Pour dressing over potatoes, add cheese, parsley and
  peppers and toss lightly. Serve warm or chilled.

Carrot Salad

3 cups finely grated carrots	710 ml
1 (8 ounce) can crushed pineapple, drained	227 g
4 tablespoons flaked coconut	60 ml
1 tablespoon sugar	15 ml

• Combine all ingredients. Toss with ⅓ cup (80 ml) mayonnaise and mix well.

• Refrigerate.

Green and White Salad

1 (16 ounce) package frozen green peas, thawed	.5 kg
1 head cauliflower, cut into bite-size pieces	
1 (8 ounce) carton sour cream	227 g
1 (1 ounce) package dry ranch-style salad dressing	28 g

• In large bowl, combine peas and cauliflower.

• Combine sour cream and salad dressing. Toss with vegetables.

• Refrigerate.

Marinated Cucumbers

⅓ cup vinegar	80 ml
2 tablespoons sugar	30 ml
1 teaspoon dried dillweed	5 ml
3 cucumbers, peeled, sliced	

• Combine vinegar, sugar, 1 teaspoon (5 ml) salt, dill weed and ¼ teaspoon (1 ml) pepper. Pour over cucumbers.

• Refrigerate 1 hour before serving.

• • •

Cucumber Salad

1 (3 ounce) package lime gelatin	84 g
2 medium cucumbers	
1 tablespoon minced onion	15 ml
½ cup mayonnaise	120 ml
½ cup sour cream	120 ml

• Dissolve gelatin in ¾ cup (180 ml) boiling water and mix well. Bring to room temperature.

• Slice cucumber in half and remove seeds. Grate cucumber and add to cool gelatin with onion, mayonnaise and sour cream.

• Pour into square dish. Refrigerate until set.

• • •

Calypso Coleslaw

1 (16 ounce) package shredded cabbage	.5 kg
1 bunch green onions with tops, sliced	
2 cups cubed cheddar or mozzarella cheese	480 ml
¼ cup sliced ripe olives	60 ml
1 (15 ounce) can whole kernel corn with	
peppers, drained	425 g

• Combine all slaw ingredients and add a few sprinkles of salt.

Dressing for Calypso Coleslaw

1 cup mayonnaise	240 ml
2 tablespoons sugar	30 ml
1 tablespoon prepared mustard	15 ml
2 tablespoons vinegar	30 ml

• Combine dressing ingredients and mix well.

• Add dressing to slaw, toss, cover and refrigerate.

● ● ●

Terrific Tortellini Salad

2 (14 ounce) packages frozen cheese tortellini   2 (396 g)
2 bell peppers: 1 green and 1 red, diced
1 cucumber, chopped
1 (14 ounce) can artichoke hearts, rinsed, drained   396 g
1 (8 ounce) bottle creamy Caesar salad dressing   227 g

• Prepare tortellini according to package directions and drain. Rinse with cold water, drain and chill.

• Combine tortellini, bell peppers, cucumber, artichoke hearts and dressing in large bowl. (You may want to add a little black pepper).

• Cover and refrigerate at least 2 hours before serving.

• • •

Chicken Salad

3 cups chicken breast halves, cooked, finely
    chopped   710 ml
1½ cups chopped celery   360 ml
½ cup sweet pickle relish   120 ml
2 hard-boiled eggs, chopped
¾ cup mayonnaise   180 ml

• Combine all ingredients and several sprinkles of salt and pepper.

Tip: Adding ½ cup (120 ml) chopped pecans gives the chicken salad a special taste.

• • •

Fusilli Pasta Salad

1 (16 ounce) package fusilli or corkscrew pasta	.5 kg
1 (16 ounce) package frozen broccoli-cauliflower combination	.5 kg
1 (8 ounce) package cubed mozzarella cheese	227 g
1 (8 ounce) bottle of Catalina salad dressing	227 g

• Cook pasta according to package directions. Drain and cool.

• Cook vegetables in microwave according to package directions. Drain and cool.

• In large bowl, combine pasta, vegetables and cheese chunks. Toss with Catalina dressing. Refrigerate several hours before serving.

Color-Coded Salad

1 (16 ounce) package tri-colored macaroni, cooked, drained	.5 kg
1 red bell pepper, julienne	
1 cup chopped zucchini	240 ml
1 cup broccoli florets	240 ml

• Combine all ingredients.

• Toss with 1 cup (240 ml) Caesar salad dressing. Refrigerate.

Fantastic Fruit Salad

2 (11 ounce) cans mandarin oranges	2 (312 g)
2 (15 ounce) cans pineapple chunks	2 (425 g)
1 (16 ounce) carton frozen strawberries, thawed	.5 kg
1 (20 ounce) can peach pie filling	567 g
1 (20 ounce) can apricot pie filling	567 g

• Drain oranges, pineapple and strawberries. Combine all ingredients and fold together gently. (If you like, add 2 sliced bananas to salad.)

Cherry Salad

1 (20 ounce) can cherry pie filling	567 g
1 (20 ounce) can crushed pineapple, drained	567 g
1 (14 ounce) can sweetened condensed milk	396 g
1 cup miniature marshmallows	240 ml
1 cup chopped pecans	240 ml
1 (8 ounce) carton whipped topping	227 g

• In large bowl, combine pie filling, pineapple, condensed milk, marshmallows and pecans.

• Fold in whipped topping, chill and serve in pretty crystal bowl. (You may add a couple drops of red food coloring if you like a brighter color.)

• • • • • • • • • •

Butter Mint Salad

1 (6 ounce) box lime gelatin	168 g
1 (20 ounce) can crushed pineapple with juice	567 g
½ (10 ounce) bag miniature marshmallows	½ (280 g)
1 (8 ounce) carton whipped topping	227 g
1 (8 ounce) bag butter mints, crushed	227 g

• Pour dry gelatin over pineapple, stir in marshmallows and set overnight. Fold in whipped topping and butter mints. Pour into 9 x 13-inch (23 x 33 cm) dish and freeze.

● ● ●

Creamy Fruit Salad

This will get you requests for more – it's so easy, you can oblige!

1 (14 ounce) can sweetened, condensed milk	396 g
¼ cup lemon juice	60 ml
1 (20 ounce) can peach pie filling	567 g
1 (15 ounce) can pineapple chunks, drained	425 g
2 (15 ounce) cans fruit cocktail, drained	2 (425 g)
1 cup chopped pecans	240 ml
1 (8 ounce) carton whipped topping	227 g

• In large bowl, combine condensed milk and lemon juice and stir well. Add pie filling, pineapple chunks, fruit cocktail and pecans and mix. Fold in whipped topping.

• Serve in a crystal bowl. Serves 12 to 14.

Tip: You may substitute any pie filling.

Soups
and
Stews

Potato and Ham Chowder

1 carrot, grated	
2 ribs celery, sliced	
1 onion, chopped	
1 (4.5 ounce) package julienne potato mix	128 g
3 cups milk	710 ml
2 cups cooked, cubed ham	480 ml
Grated sharp cheddar cheese for garnish	

• In soup kettle, combine 2¾ cups (660 ml) water with carrot, celery, onion and potato mix package. Bring to boil, reduce heat, cover and simmer 20 minutes.

• Stir in milk and packet of sauce with potatoes, mix, stir well and return to boiling. Simmer 2 minutes. Stir in ham. When serving, garnish with sharp cheddar cheese.

Italian Vegetable Soup

1 pound bulk Italian sausage	.5 kg
2 onions, chopped	
2 teaspoons minced garlic	10 ml
1 (1 ounce) envelope Beefy Recipe soup mix	28 g
1 (15 ounce) can sliced carrots, drained	425 g
2 (15 ounce) cans Italian stewed tomatoes	2 (425 g)
2 (15 ounce) cans garbanzo beans, drained	2 (425 g)
1 cup elbow macaroni	240 ml

• In large soup kettle, brown sausage, onions and garlic. Pour off fat and add 4 cups (1 L) water, soup mix, carrots, tomatoes and garbanzo beans. Bring to boil, reduce heat to low and simmer for 25 minutes. Add elbow macaroni and continue cooking another 15 to 20 minutes or until macaroni is tender.

Chicken and Rice Gumbo

3 (14 ounce) cans chicken broth	3 (396 g)
1 pound boneless, skinless chicken, cubed	.5 kg
2 (15 ounce) cans whole kernel corn, drained	2 (425 g)
2 (15 ounce) cans stewed tomatoes with liquid	2 (425 g)
¾ cup uncooked white rice	180 ml
1 teaspoon Cajun seasoning	5 ml
2 (10 ounce) packages frozen okra, thawed, chopped	2 (280 g)

- In soup kettle on high heat, combine chicken broth and chicken pieces and cook 15 minutes.
- Add remaining ingredients plus 1 teaspoon (5 ml) pepper and bring to boil. Reduce heat and simmer for 20 minutes or until rice is done.

• • •

Ham and Veggie Chowder

1 cup chopped onion	240 ml
1 cup chopped celery	240 ml
3 cups shredded cabbage	710 ml
3 cups cooked, cubed ham	710 ml
2 (15 ounce) cans Mexican-style stewed tomatoes	2 (425 g)
1 (15 ounce) can whole kernel corn, drained	425 g
1 (15 ounce) can whole new potatoes, sliced	425 g
2 (14 ounce) cans chicken broth	2 (396 g)
½ cup ketchup	120 ml
¼ cup packed light brown sugar	60 ml

- Saute onion and celery in large soup kettle with a little oil, over medium-high heat saute onion and celery.
- Add remaining ingredients and bring to boil. Reduce heat and simmer for 1 hour.

Ham and Lentil Stew

1 (1 ounce) envelope Onion-Mushroom Recipe soup mix	28 g
1 (14 ounce) can chicken broth	396 g
1 cup lentils, rinsed, drained	240 ml
1 cup uncooked brown rice	240 ml
2 cups chopped onions	480 ml
2 cups chopped celery	480 ml
2 (15 ounce) cans whole tomatoes with liquid	2 (425 g)
1 (15 ounce) can sliced carrots	425 g
2 cups cooked, cubed ham	480 ml
1 tablespoon apple cider vinegar	15 ml

• In soup kettle, combine soup mix, chicken broth, lentils, rice, onions, celery and 2 cups (480 ml) water. Bring to boil, reduce heat to medium and simmer for 45 minutes.

• On medium heat, stir in tomatoes, carrots, ham and vinegar and cook until mixture is thoroughly hot.

● ● ●

Chili-Soup Warmer

1 (10 ounce) can tomato-bisque soup	280 g
1 (10 ounce) can chili	280 g
1 (10 ounce) can fiesta chili-beef soup	280 g
1 (15 ounce) can chicken broth	425 g

• In saucepan, combine all soups and broth. Add amount of water to produce desired thickness of soup.

• Heat and serve hot with crackers.

Ham and Corn Chowder

3 medium potatoes, cubed	
2 (14 ounce) cans chicken broth, divided	2 (396 g)
2 ribs celery, chopped	
1 onion, chopped	
4 tablespoons flour	60 ml
1 pint half-and-half cream	.5 kg
½ teaspoon cayenne pepper	2 ml
1 (15 ounce) can whole kernel corn	425 g
1 (15 ounce) can cream-style corn	425 g
3 cups cooked, cubed ham	710 ml
1 (8 ounce) package shredded processed cheese	227 g

• Cook potatoes in 1 can chicken broth. In large soup kettle with little oil, saute celery and onion. On medium heat, add flour and mix well. Add second can broth and half-and-half; cook stirring constantly until mixture thickens.

• Add potatoes, cayenne pepper, corn, cream-style corn, ham, cheese and salt and pepper to taste. Heat slowly. Stir several times to keep from sticking.

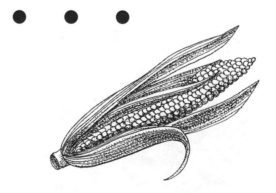

A Different Chili

2 onions, coarsely chopped
3 (15 ounce) cans great Northern beans, drained   3 (425 g)
2 (14 ounce) cans chicken broth   2 (396 g)
2 tablespoons minced garlic   30 ml
1 (7 ounce) can chopped green chilies   198 g
1 tablespoon ground cumin   15 ml
3 cups cooked, finely chopped chicken breasts   710 ml
1 (8 ounce) package shredded Monterey
Jack cheese   227 g

• In large, heavy pot with little oil, cook onions about 5 minutes, but do not brown. Place 1 can beans in shallow bowl and mash with fork.

• Add mashed beans, 2 remaining cans of beans, chicken broth, garlic, green chilies and cumin. Bring to boil, reduce heat, cover and simmer 30 minutes.

• Add chopped chicken (or deli turkey), stir to blend well and heat until chili is thoroughly hot. When serving, top each bowl with 3 tablespoons (45 ml) cheese.

● ● ●

Chicken and Vegetable Chili

1 (16 ounce) package frozen, chopped onions and bell peppers	.5 kg
2 tablespoons minced garlic	30 ml
2 tablespoons chili powder	30 ml
3 teaspoons ground cumin	15 ml
2 pounds chicken cutlets, cubed	1 kg
2 (14 ounce) cans chicken broth	2 (396 g)
3 (15 ounce) cans pinto beans with jalapenos, divided	3 (425 g)

• Cook onions and bell peppers about 5 minutes in large, heavy pot over medium-high heat with little oil and stir occasionally,

• Add garlic, chili powder, cumin and cubed chicken and cook another 5 minutes. Stir in broth and a little salt. Bring to boil, reduce heat, cover and simmer for 15 minutes.

• Place 1 can beans in shallow bowl and mash with fork. Add mashed beans and remaining 2 cans of beans to pot. Bring to boil, reduce heat and simmer for 10 minutes.

Tip: Delicious served with hot, buttered flour tortillas or spooned over small, original corn chips.

● ● ●

Soups

• • • • • • • • • •

Ham and Sausage Stew

3 cups cooked, diced ham	710 ml
1 pound Polish sausage, sliced	.5 kg
3 (14 ounce) cans chicken broth	3 (396 g)
2 (15 ounce) cans Mexican stewed tomatoes	2 (425 g)
2 teaspoons ground cumin	10 ml
1 teaspoon cocoa	5 ml
1 teaspoon dried oregano	5 ml
2 (15 ounce) cans pinto beans with liquid	2 (425 g)
2 (15 ounce) cans whole kernel corn, drained	2 (425 g)
Flour tortillas	

• In large roaster, combine ham, sausage, chicken broth, tomatoes, cumin, cocoa, oregano and salt to taste. On high heat, bring to boil and cook for 5 minutes.

• Add pinto beans and corn, reduce heat and simmer for 35 minutes. Serve with warmed, buttered flour tortillas.

● ● ●

Navy Bean Soup

3 (15 ounce) cans navy beans with liquid	3 (425 g)
1 cup chopped ham	240 ml
1 large onion, chopped	
½ teaspoon garlic powder	2 ml

• In large saucepan, combine beans, ham, onion and garlic powder.

• Add 1 cup (240 ml) water and bring to boil. Simmer until onion is tender crisp. Serve hot with cornbread.

Hearty Bean and Ham Soup

¼ cup (½ stick) butter	60 ml
1 (15 ounce) can sliced carrots, drained	425 g
1 cup chopped celery	240 ml
1 cup chopped green bell pepper	240 ml
2 - 3 cups cooked, diced ham*	480 ml
2 (15 ounce) cans navy beans with liquid	2 (425 g)
2 (15 ounce) cans jalapeno pinto beans with liquid	2 (425 g)
2 (14 ounce) cans chicken broth	2 (396 g)
2 teaspoons chili powder	10 ml

• In kettle or soup pot with butter, cook carrots, celery and bell pepper about 8 minutes until tender-crisp. Add diced ham, navy beans, pinto beans, chicken broth, chili powder and salt and pepper to taste. Boil, stirring constantly, for 3 minutes. Reduce heat and simmer for 15 minutes.

Tip: *What a great supper for a cold winter night and a pan of hot cornbread would be just the thing to top it off!*

(Use 2 (8 ounce/227 g) packages corn muffin mix. This mix only needs 2 eggs and ²/₃ cup/160 ml milk.)

* *This is a great way to use that leftover ham or just buy it at the deli.*

Soups

Tortilla Soup

3 - 4 flour tortillas
1 (1.8 ounce) package Knorr Tomato with
  Basil soup mix   57 g
1 (14 ounce) can chicken broth   396 g
2 cups salsa   480 ml
1 (10 ounce) can enchilada sauce   280 g
2 cups cooked, diced chicken breast   480 ml
1 avocado, sliced
1 (8 ounce) package shredded Monterey
  Jack cheese   227 g

- Preheat oven to 325° (162° C). Cut tortillas in thin strips and bake for 10 to 15 minutes or until crisp. In large saucepan, combine soup mix, broth, salsa, enchilada sauce and 1 cup (240 ml) water. Bring to boil, stirring constantly, and stir in diced chicken. Serve in shallow bowls.

- Place diced avocado, cheese and toasted tortilla strips in separate bowls so each person can garnish as they wish.

Tip: Leftover rotisserie chicken can substitute for chicken breasts.

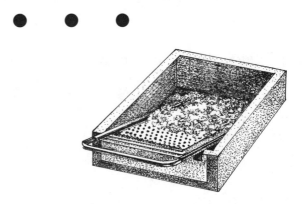

Veggies
and
Sides

Pasta Frittata

¼ cup (½ stick) butter	60 ml
1 onion, chopped	
1 red bell pepper, chopped	
1 green bell pepper, chopped	
1 (8 ounce) package thin spaghetti,	
slightly broken, cooked	227 g
1 (12 ounce) package shredded mozzarella	
cheese, divided	340 g
5 eggs	
1 cup milk	240 ml
2 teaspoons dried basil	10 ml
2 teaspoons oregano	10 ml

• Preheat oven to 375° (190° C). In skillet with butter, saute onion and bell peppers, but do not brown. In large bowl, combine onion mixture, spaghetti, half mozzarella cheese and salt and pepper to taste. Toss.

• In separate bowl, beat eggs, milk, seasonings and remaining cheese. Stir in spaghetti mixture and pour in greased 9 x 13-inch (23 x 33 cm) baking dish. Cover and bake 20 minutes. Uncover and make sure eggs are set, if not, cook 4 or 5 more minutes.

Tip: Great served with rotisserie chicken, from the grocery store.

Unforgettable Tortellini Bake

1 (18 ounce) package frozen cheese tortellini, cooked, drained	510 g
1 (16 ounce) package frozen chopped broccoli, thawed, drained	.5 kg
1 (4 ounce) jar sliced pimentos	114 g
1 onion, chopped	
1 bell pepper, chopped	
2 (10 ounce) cans cream of chicken soup	2 (280 g)
1 teaspoon minced garlic	5 ml
1 teaspoon Italian seasoning	5 ml
1 (8 ounce) package shredded mozzarella cheese, divided	227 g

- Preheat oven to 350° (176° C). In large bowl, combine tortellini, broccoli, pimentos, onion, bell pepper, soup, garlic and Italian seasoning. Mix well. Fold in half cheese and pour into greased 3-quart (3 L) baking dish. Cover and bake 45 minutes.

- Remove from oven, sprinkle remaining cheese over top and return to oven for 5 minutes.

• • • • • • • • • • •

Confetti Orzo

¾ cup orzo pasta	180 ml
½ cup (1 stick) butter	120 ml
1 (12 ounce) package frozen broccoli florets, thawed	340 g
1 bunch fresh green onions, chopped	
1 red bell pepper, chopped	
1 green bell pepper, chopped	
2 teaspoons minced garlic	10 ml
2 teaspoons chicken bouillon	10 ml
1 (16 ounce) jar creamy alfredo sauce	.5 kg

• Preheat oven to 325° (162° C). Cook orzo according to package directions. Drain. Cook butter, broccoli, onions, bell peppers and garlic in large skillet on medium heat for 10 to 15 minutes, until tender-crisp.

• Spoon into large bowl, combine broccoli mixture, orzo, chicken bouillon and alfredo sauce and mix well. Cover and bake for 30 minutes. If you like, add 3 cups (710 ml) cooked, cubed chicken to casserole.

● ● ●

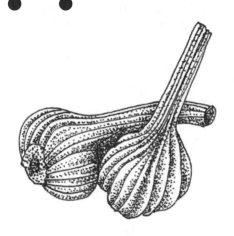

California-Rice Casserole

¼ cup (½ stick) butter	60 ml
1 onion, chopped	
1 green bell pepper, chopped	
1 red bell pepper, chopped	
4 cups cooked instant white rice	1 L
2 (8 ounce) cartons sour cream	2 (227 g)
1 cup small curd cottage cheese, drained	240 ml
1 (7 ounce) can chopped green chilies	198 g
1 (8 ounce) package shredded sharp cheddar cheese	227 g

• Preheat oven to 350° (176° C). In large saucepan with butter, saute onion and bell peppers until golden, but not brown. Stir in rice, sour cream, cottage cheese and salt to taste.

• Place half rice mixture in greased 9 x 13-inch (23 x 33 cm) baking dish. Spread green chilies and half cheese over rice mixture. Spoon remaining rice mixture on casserole and top with remaining cheese.

• Bake uncovered for 30 minutes or until hot and bubbly.

Tip: This is great served with rotisserie chicken, from the grocery store.

● ● ●

Vegetable Frittata

1 onion, chopped	
1 green bell pepper, chopped	
1 red bell pepper, chopped	
2 cups chopped zucchini	480 ml
2 cups chopped yellow squash	480 ml
⅓ cup half-and-half cream	80 ml
1 (8 ounce) package cream cheese, softened	227 g
6 large eggs, beaten	
1½ cups shredded mozzarella cheese	360 ml
1 teaspoon garlic powder	5 ml
1 cup seasoned breadcrumbs	240 ml

• Preheat oven to 350° (176° C). In large skillet with little oil, cook onion, bell peppers, zucchini and squash just until tender-crisp. Drain and set aside.

• In mixing bowl, beat cream and cream cheese until creamy. Add eggs and cheese. Beat until they blend well. Mix by hand and fold in garlic, 1 teaspoon (5 ml) salt and breadcrumbs.

• Add vegetables to mixture; pour into greased 9-inch (23 cm) springform pan and bake 55 minutes or until center sets and browns lightly. Let stand 10 minutes before removing sides and slicing.

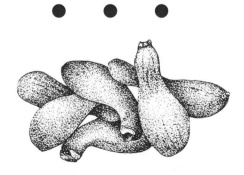

• • • • • • • • • •

Posh Squash

8 medium yellow squash, sliced
½ green bell pepper, seeded, chopped
1 small onion, chopped
1 (8 ounce) package cubed Mexican processed
    cheese   227 g

• Combine squash, bell pepper and onion in large
  saucepan and just barely cover with water.

• Cook just until tender, about 10 to 15 minutes.

• Drain and add cheese. Stir until cheese melts and
  pour into buttered 2-quart (2 L) baking dish.

• Bake at 350° (176° C) for 15 minutes.

● ● ●

Zucchini Beau Monde

6 - 8 medium zucchini, sliced
1 teaspoon beau monde seasoning   5 ml
1 (8 ounce) carton sour cream   227 g
¼ cup grated parmesan cheese   60 ml

• Saute zucchini in 2 tablespoons (30 ml) butter. Cook
  on low for about 5 minutes.

• Stir in seasoning, sour cream and cheese. Heat but do
  not boil.

● ● ●

• • • • • • • • • •

Super Corn Casserole

1 (15 ounce) can whole kernel corn	425 g
1 (15 ounce) can cream-style corn	425 g
½ cup (1 stick) butter, melted	120 ml
1 (8 ounce) carton sour cream	227 g
1 (6 ounce) package Jalapeno cornbread mix	168 g

• Mix all ingredients and pour into greased 9 x 13-inch (23 x 33 cm) baking dish.

• Bake uncovered at 350° (176° C) for 35 minutes.

• • •

Stuffed Corn

1 (15 ounce) cans cream-style corn	425 g
1 (15 ounce) can whole kernel corn, drained	425 g
½ cup (1 stick) butter, melted	120 ml
1 (6 ounce) package chicken stuffing mix	168 g

• Combine all ingredients plus seasoning packet and ½ cup (120 ml) water and mix well.

• Spoon into buttered 9 x 13-inch (23 x 33 cm) baking pan. Bake at 350° (176° C) for 30 minutes.

• • •

Shoe-Peg Corn

1 (8 ounce) package cream cheese, softened	227 g
½ cup (1 stick) butter, softened	120 ml
3 (15 ounce) cans shoe-peg corn	3 (425 g)
1 (4 ounce) can chopped green chilies	114 g

• With mixer or fork, combine butter and cream cheese. Add corn and green chilies and mix well.

• Spoon into 7 x 11-inch (18 x 28 cm) greased casserole.

• Bake covered at 350° (176° C) for 30 minutes.

Corn Pudding

1 (8 ounce) package corn muffin mix	227 g
1 (15 ounce) can cream-style corn	425 g
½ cup sour cream	120 ml
3 eggs, slightly beaten	

• Combine all ingredients and pour into buttered 2-quart (2 L) baking dish.

• Bake uncovered at 350° (176° C) for about 35 minutes.

• • • • • • • • • • •

Classic Baked Bean Stand-By

3 (18 ounce) cans Bush's baked beans   3 (510 g)
½ cup chili sauce   120 ml
⅓ cup packed brown sugar   80 ml
4 slices bacon, cooked, crumbled

- In buttered 3-quart (3 L) baking dish, combine baked beans, chili sauce and brown sugar.

- Bake at 325° (162° C) for 40 minutes.

- When ready to serve, sprinkle bacon on top.

● ● ●

Creamy Cabbage Bake

1 head cabbage, shredded
1 (10 ounce) can cream of celery soup   280 g
⅔ cup milk   160 ml
1 (8 ounce) package shredded cheddar cheese   227 g

- Place cabbage in 2-quart (2 L) buttered baking dish.

- Pour celery soup diluted with milk over top of cabbage. Bake covered at 325° (162° C) for 30 minutes.

- Remove from oven, sprinkle with cheese and bake uncovered another 5 minutes.

● ● ●

Chicken
Dishes

Chicken Chow Mein

3 cups cooked, cubed chicken or turkey	710 ml
2 (10 ounce) cans cream of chicken soup	2 (280 g)
2 (15 ounce) cans chop suey vegetables, drained	2 (425 g)
1 (8 ounce) can sliced water chestnuts, drained	227 g
1 onion, chopped	
1 bell pepper, chopped	
½ teaspoon hot sauce	2 ml
½ teaspoon curry powder	2 ml
1½ cups chow mein noodles	360 ml

- Preheat oven to 350° (176° C). In large bowl, combine chicken, soup, vegetables, water chestnuts, onion, bell pepper, hot sauce, curry powder and salt and pepper to taste and mix well.

- Spoon into greased 9 x 13-inch (23 x 33 cm) baking dish. Sprinkle chow mein noodles over top and bake 40 minutes.

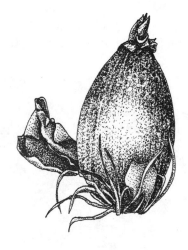

• • • • • • • • • •

Ranch Chicken To Go

1 (8 ounce) package of your favorite pasta	227 g
½ cup (1 stick) butter	120 ml
1 (10 ounce) can cream of chicken soup	280 g
1 (1 ounce) package ranch-style dressing mix	28 g
2 (15 ounce) cans peas and carrots, drained	2 (425 g)
3 cups cooked, cubed chicken or turkey	710 ml

• Preheat oven to 350° (176° C). Cook pasta according to package directions. In saucepan, combine butter, soup, dressing mix, peas and carrots. Heat, stirring occasionally, until butter melts and ingredients mix well.

• Toss with cooked pasta and chicken and spoon into greased 3-quart (3 L) baking dish. Cover and bake 25 minutes.

● ● ●

Baked Chicken Casserole

2 (10 ounce) cans cream of mushroom soup	2 (280 g)
1 soup can milk	
2 teaspoons curry powder	10 ml
1 (4 ounce) can sliced mushrooms	114 g
2½ cups cooked, instant rice	600 ml
1 (8 ounce) can green peas, drained	227 g
3 cups cooked, cubed chicken or turkey	710 ml
3 slices bacon, cooked, crumbled	

• Preheat oven to 350° (176° C). In large bowl, combine soup, milk, curry powder, mushrooms, rice, peas, chicken and bacon and mix well.

• Spoon into greased 9 x 13-inch (23 x 33 cm) baking pan. Cover and bake for 40 minutes.

• • • • • • • • • •

Chicken-Mushroom Bake

1 (4 ounce) can sliced mushrooms	114 g
1 (10 ounce) can cream of chicken soup	280 g
1 (8 ounce) carton sour cream	227 g
½ cup cooking sherry	120 ml
1 (1 ounce) envelope dry onion soup mix	28 g
2 cups cooked, cubed chicken or turkey	480 ml

• Preheat oven to 350° (176° C). In large bowl, combine mushrooms, soup, sour cream, sherry, onion soup mix and chicken. Spoon into greased 3-quart (3 L) baking dish and bake 40 minutes. Serve over hot cooked rice.

• • •

Delicious Carnival Couscous

1 (5.7 ounce) box toasted pine nut couscous	155 g
1 red bell pepper, chopped	
1 yellow squash, seeded, diced	
1 cup fresh broccoli florets, coarsely chopped	240 ml
¼ cup (½ stick) butter	60 ml
1½ cups cooked, cubed chicken breast or turkey	360 ml

• Preheat oven to 325° (162° C). Cook couscous according to package directions, but leave out butter. Saute bell pepper, squash and broccoli in saucepan, with butter. Cook about 10 minutes.

• In large bowl, combine couscous, vegetables, chicken and salt and pepper to taste. Transfer to greased 3-quart (3 L) baking dish and bake 20 minutes.

• • • • • • • • • •

Quick Chicken Supper

1 (16 ounce) package frozen broccoli	
florets, thawed	.5 kg
1 (10 ounce) can cream of chicken soup	280 g
2/3 cup mayonnaise	160 ml
1 cup shredded cheddar cheese	240 ml
3 cups cooked, cubed chicken or turkey	710 ml
2 cups crushed cheese crackers	480 ml

• Preheat oven to 350° (176° C). In large bowl, combine broccoli, soup, mayonnaise, cheese and chicken and mix well.

• Pour into greased 3-quart (3 L) baking dish. Cover and bake 25 minutes.

• Uncover and spread cheese crackers over top of casserole and return to oven for 15 minutes.

• • •

Spicy Chicken and Rice

3 cups cooked, sliced chicken	710 ml
2 cups cooked brown rice	480 ml
1 (10 ounce) can fiesta nacho cheese soup	280 g
1 (10 ounce) can chopped tomatoes and	
green chilies	280 g

• Combine chicken, rice, cheese soup, tomatoes and green chilies and mix well. Spoon mixture into buttered 3-quart (3 L) baking dish.

• Cook covered at 350° (176° C) for 45 minutes.

Chicken Taco Pie

1½ pounds boneless, skinless chicken breast halves	.7 kg
1 (1.5 ounce) package taco seasoning mix	45 g
1 green bell pepper, finely chopped	
1 red bell pepper, finely chopped	
1½ cups shredded Mexican 4-cheese blend	360 ml
1 (8 ounce) package corn muffin mix	227 g
1 egg	
⅓ cup milk	80 ml

• Preheat oven to 400° (204° C). Cut chicken into 1-inch (2.5 cm) pieces and cook on medium-high heat in large skillet with a little oil. Cook about 10 minutes and drain.

• Stir in taco seasoning, bell peppers and ¾ cup (180 ml) water. Reduce heat and simmer, stirring several times, for another 10 minutes. Spoon into buttered 9-inch, (23 cm), deep-dish pie pan and sprinkle with cheese.

• Prepare corn muffin mix with egg and milk and mix well. Spoon over top of pie and bake for 20 minutes or until top is golden brown. Let stand about 5 minutes before serving.

• • •

Creamy Tarragon Chicken

1½ cups flour	360 ml
6 boneless, skinless chicken breast halves	
2 tablespoons oil	30 ml
1 (14 ounce) can chicken broth	396 g
1 cup milk	240 ml
2 teaspoons dried tarragon	10 ml
1 (4 ounce) can sliced mushrooms, drained	114 g
2 (8 ounce) packages Roasted Chicken Rice*	2 (227 g)

• Mix flour and little salt and pepper on waxed paper and coat chicken. Save extra flour. Heat oil in large skillet over medium-high heat and cook chicken breasts, turning once, about 10 minutes or until light brown. Transfer to plate.

• In same skillet, stir in 2 tablespoons (30 ml) flour-salt mixture. Whisk in chicken broth, milk and tarragon and heat, stirring constantly, until bubbly. Add mushrooms and return chicken to skillet. Cover and simmer for 10 to 15 minutes or until sauce thickens.

* Microwave rice according to package directions and place on serving platter. Spoon chicken and sauce over rice.

● ● ●

• • • • • • • • • • •

Stir-Fry Chicken and Veggies

1¼ cups instant rice	300 ml
¼ cup (½ stick) butter	60 ml
1½ pounds chicken tenderloin strips	.7 kg
1 (16 ounce) package frozen broccoli, cauliflower and carrots	.5 kg
2 sweet red bell peppers, cored, julienned	
½ cup stir-fry sauce	120 ml

• Cook rice according to package directions and keep warm. In large non-stick skillet, melt butter and stir-fry chicken strips about 5 minutes or until light brown.

• Stir in vegetables and cook 8 minutes longer. Pour in stir-fry sauce and mix well. Cover and cook 2 minutes or until thoroughly hot. Serve over hot cooked rice.

● ● ●

• • • • • • • • • •

Tri-Color Pasta with Turkey Supper

1 (12 ounce) package tri-color spiral pasta	340 g
1 (4 ounce) can sliced ripe olives, drained	114 g
1 cup fresh broccoli florets	240 ml
1 cup cauliflower florets	240 ml
2 small yellow squash, sliced	
1 cup halved cherry tomatoes	240 ml
1 (8 ounce) bottle Cheddar-Parmesan Ranch dressing	227 g
Slices from 1½ pound Hickory Smoked Cracked Pepper turkey breast	.7 kg

• Cook pasta according to package directions. Drain and rinse in cold water. Place in large salad bowl and add olives, broccoli, cauliflower, sliced squash and tomatoes. Toss with dressing.

• Place thin slices of turkey breast, arranged in a row, over salad. Serve immediately.

• • •

• • • • • • • • • •

Lemony Chicken and Noodles

1 (8 ounce) package wide egg noodles	227 g
1 (10 ounce) package frozen sugar snap peas, thawed	280 g
1 (14 ounce) can chicken broth	396 g
1 teaspoon fresh grated lemon peel	5 ml
2 cups cubed skinless rotisserie chicken meat	480 ml
½ cup whipping cream	120 ml

• In large saucepan with boiling water, cook noodles according to package directions, but add snap peas to noodles 1 minute before noodles are done. Drain and return to saucepan.

• Add chicken broth, lemon peel, chicken pieces and ½ teaspoon (2 ml) each of salt and pepper. Heat, stirring constantly, until thoroughly hot. Over low heat, gently stir in heavy cream. Serve hot.

● ● ●

Roasted Chicken with Red Peppers

1 (14 ounce) can chicken broth	396 g
1 (8 ounce) can whole kernel corn, drained	227 g
2 cups cooked, cubed chicken breast	480 ml
1 (5 ounce) box couscous	143 g
1 cup roasted red bell peppers	240 ml
¼ cup toasted pine nuts	60 ml

• In saucepan over medium-high heat, combine chicken broth, corn, chicken, couscous and roasted bell peppers. Cover and simmer about 3 minutes.

• Transfer to serving dish and sprinkle pine nuts over top.

Vermicelli Toss

1 (10 ounce) package vermicelli	280 g
1 (10 ounce) package frozen sugar snap peas	280 g
2 tablespoons butter	30 ml
3 cups rotisserie-cooked chicken strips	710 ml
1 (11 ounce) can mandarin oranges, drained	312 g
⅔ cup stir-fry sauce	160 ml

• Cook vermicelli according to package directions. Stir in sugar snap peas and cook 1 additional minute. Drain and stir in butter until butter melts. Spoon into bowl.

• Add chicken strips, oranges and stir-fry sauce. Toss.

Chilly Night's Turkey Bake

1 (6 ounce) package chicken stuffing mix	168 g
1½ pounds deli turkey, cut into (1-inch/2.5 cm) strips	.7 kg
1 (10 ounce) can cream of chicken soup	280 g
½ cup sour cream	120 ml
1 (16 ounce) bag frozen mixed vegetables, thawed, drained	.5 kg

• Preheat oven to 375° (190° C). Sprinkle ½ cup (120 ml) dry stuffing mix evenly over bottom of greased 9 x 13-inch (23 x 33 cm) baking dish. Set aside.

• In bowl, combine remaining stuffing and 1 cup (240 ml) water; stir just until moist and set aside.

• Place turkey strips over dry stuffing mix in baking dish. In bowl, mix soup, sour cream and vegetables, spoon over turkey strips and top with prepared stuffing.

• Bake uncovered for 25 minutes.

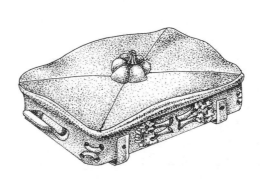

Turkey and Cornbread Casserole

3 celery ribs, chopped	
1 onion, chopped	
3 cups packed crumbled cornbread	710 ml
1 tablespoon poultry seasoning	15 ml
4 cups cooked deli turkey, cubed	1 L
1 (14 ounce) can chicken broth	396 g
1 (8 ounce) carton sour cream	227 g
1 egg, lightly beaten	
1 (4 ounce) can sliced mushrooms, drained	114 g
¼ cup (½ stick) butter, melted	60 ml
1½ cups shredded cheddar cheese	360 ml

- Preheat oven to 350° (176° C). In skillet with little oil, saute celery and onion until tender, but not brown. In large bowl, combine crumbled cornbread and poultry seasoning and layer half cornbread on greased 7 x 11-inch (18 x 28 cm) baking dish.

- Combine celery-onion mixture, cubed turkey, chicken broth, sour cream, egg and mushrooms and spoon mixture evenly over top of cornbread mixture.

- Drizzle with melted butter and bake uncovered for 30 minutes. Remove from oven, sprinkle cheese over top and return to oven for about 5 minutes.

• • • • • • • • • • •

Chicken-Waldorf Salad

1 pound boneless, skinless chicken breasts	.5 kg
1 red apple, with peel, sliced	
1 green apple, with peel, sliced	
1 cup sliced celery	240 ml
½ cup chopped walnuts	120 ml
2 (6 ounce) cartons orange yogurt	2 (168 g)
½ cup mayonnaise	120 ml
1 (6 ounce) package shredded lettuce	168 g

• Place chicken in large saucepan and cover with water. On high heat, cook about 15 minutes. Drain and cool. Cut chicken into 1-inch (2.5 cm) chunks and season with salt and pepper. Place in large salad bowl.

• Add sliced apples, celery and walnuts. Stir in yogurt and mayonnaise. Toss to mix well and serve at room temperature or chilled. Serve over shredded lettuce.

● ● ●

Southwest Pizza

No need to order pizza when you have all the "makings" in the pantry and freezer – and this is a deliciously "different" pizza, that's sure to please.

1 (12-inch/32 cm) pre-baked pizza crust
¾ cup prepared guacamole   180 ml
1 (10 ounce) package cooked, Southwest-style
   chicken breast   280 g
½ cup roasted red peppers, drained, sliced   120 ml
1 (4 ounce) can sliced ripe olives   114 g
1 (8 ounce) package shredded Mexican
   4-cheese blend   227 g

• Preheat oven to 350° (176° C). Place pizza crust on greased cookie sheet and spread guacamole over crust. Top with chicken, red peppers and olives and spread evenly. Top with cheese.

• Bake 15 minutes or just until cheese bubbles and is slightly brown. Cut pizza into wedges to serve.

Taco Chicken Over Spanish Rice

All this needs for a great supper is a tossed salad with slices of avocado and tossed with a honey-mustard dressing and a few hot, buttered flour tortillas to top that off!

1¼ cups flour	300 ml
2 (1 ounce) envelopes taco seasoning	2 (28 g)
2 large eggs, beaten	
8 boneless, skinless chicken breast halves	
2 (15 ounce) cans Spanish rice	2 (425 g)
1 cup shredded Mexican 4-cheese blend	240 ml

- Preheat oven to 350° (176° C). Place flour and taco seasoning in large shallow bowl. Place eggs and 3 tablespoons (45 ml) water in another shallow bowl and beat.

- Dip each chicken breast in egg mixture. Dredge in flour-taco mixture and press to apply lots of flour mixture. Place in greased 10 x 15-inch (25 x 38 cm) baking pan and arrange so that chicken pieces do not touch. Bake 55 to 60 minutes or until juices run clear.

- About 10 minutes before chicken is done, place Spanish rice in saucepan and stir in cheese. Heat, stirring constantly, just until cheese melts. Spoon onto serving platter and place chicken pieces over hot rice.

Zesty Orange Chicken

½ cup white wine	120 ml
½ cup orange juice concentrate	120 ml
½ cup orange marmalade	120 ml
½ teaspoon ground ginger	2 ml
½ teaspoon cinnamon	2 ml
1 large fryer chicken, quartered	
2 (11 ounce) cans mandarin oranges, drained	2 (312 g)
½ cup green grapes, halved	120 ml
1½ cups instant brown rice, cooked	360 ml

- Preheat oven to 325° (162° C). Combine wine, orange juice concentrate, marmalade, ginger and cinnamon in greased 9 x 13-inch (23 x 33 cm) baking dish. Add chicken quarters and turn to coat chicken.

- Bake uncovered, basting occasionally, for 40 minutes. Add oranges and grapes to dish during last 5 minutes of cooking.

- Serve over hot cooked and buttered rice.

• • • • • • • • • • •

Alfredo Chicken Vermicelli

1 (8 ounce) package vermicelli, broken in thirds	227 g
2 teaspoons minced garlic	10 ml
1 (16 ounce) jar alfredo sauce	.5 kg
¼ cup milk	60 ml
1 (10 ounce) box frozen broccoli florets, thawed	280 g
2 cups cooked, diced chicken	480 ml

• Cook vermicelli according to package directions and drain. Place back in saucepan, stir in garlic, alfredo sauce and milk and mix well.

• Add drained broccoli florets, cook on medium heat about 5 minutes and stir several times or until broccoli is tender. Add more milk if mixture gets too dry.

• Stir in diced chicken and spoon into serving bowl.

Tip: If you would like to garnish, sprinkle a little shredded mozzarella cheese on top.

●   ●   ●

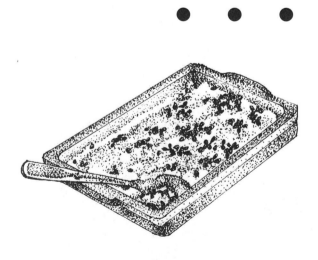

Chicken Couscous

1¼ cups chicken broth	300 ml
1 (5.6 ounce) package pine nut couscous mix	155 g
1 rotisserie chicken, boned, cut up	
1 (4 ounce) can chopped pimento	114 g
½ cup crumbled feta cheese	120 ml
1 (10 ounce) package frozen green peas, optional	280 g
1 tablespoon dried basil	15 ml
1 tablespoon lemon juice	15 ml

• Heat broth and seasoning packet from couscous in microwave on HIGH for 4 minutes or until broth begins to boil. Place couscous in large bowl and stir in broth. Cover and let stand 5 minutes.

• Fluff couscous with fork and add chicken, pimento, cheese, peas, basil and lemon juice. Toss to blend well. Serve warm.

Tip: Couscous is a quick alternative to rice or pasta and it couldn't be easier to make. All you have to do is add boiling water.

• • • • • • • • • •

Chicken-Pasta Supper Supreme

1 (10 ounce) package angel hair pasta	280 g
1 onion, chopped	
1 red bell pepper, seeded, chopped	
2 teaspoons minced garlic	10 ml
1 (10 ounce) package fresh baby spinach	280 g
2 tomatoes, chopped, drained	
3 cups cooked, chopped chicken breasts	710 ml
2 tablespoons, cooked, crumbled bacon	30 ml
½ (8 ounce) bottle creamy Italian salad dressing	½ (227 g)
¼ cup crumbled feta cheese	60 ml

• Cook angle hair pasta according to package directions. Drain and set aside.

• In large skillet with little oil, saute onion, bell pepper and garlic. Add spinach and ¼ cup (60 ml) water. Cover and cook 3 minutes or until spinach wilts. Stir in tomatoes, chicken, bacon and salad dressing and cook until mixture heats thoroughly.

• Place pasta on serving platter and spoon chicken mixture over pasta. Sprinkle with feta cheese.

Tip: Leftover chicken or deli turkey may be substituted for chicken breasts.

● ● ●

• • • • • • • • • •

Medley of Chicken and Vegetables

¼ cup (½ stick) butter	60 ml
¼ cup flour	60 ml
1 pint half-and-half cream	.5 kg
1 (10 ounce) can cream of chicken soup	280 g
1 (10 ounce) package frozen broccoli florets, thawed	280 g
1 (10 ounce) package frozen cauliflower, thawed	280 g
1 sweet red bell pepper, seeded, julienned	
1 cup cooked brown rice	240 ml
3 - 4 cups cooked, cubed chicken or turkey	710 ml
1 (8 ounce) package shredded cheddar cheese	227 g
1½ cups crushed potato chips	360 ml

• Preheat oven 325° (162° C). In large skillet, melt butter, add flour and stir until they blend. Slowly stir in cream and cook stirring constantly, until mixture thickens. Blend in soup and set aside.

• Place broccoli, cauliflower and bell pepper into greased 9 x 13-inch (23 x 33 cm) baking dish. Cover with cooked rice, half sauce and top with cubed chicken. Stir cheese into remaining sauce and pour over chicken.

• Sprinkle crushed potato chips over top of casserole and bake 40 minutes or until casserole heats thoroughly and chips are light brown.

● ● ●

Luncheon Chicken Pie

1 (12 ounce) package shredded cheddar cheese, divided	340 g
1 (10 ounce) package frozen peas and carrots, thawed	280 g
½ onion, chopped	
1 red bell pepper, seeded, chopped	
2 cups cooked, finely diced chicken breasts	480 ml
1½ cups half-and-half cream	360 ml
3 eggs	
¾ cup baking mix	180 ml

- In large bowl, combine 2 cups (480 ml) cheese, peas and carrots, onion, bell pepper and chicken. Spread into buttered 10-inch (25 cm) deep-dish pie plate.

- In mixing bowl, beat cream, eggs, baking mix and salt and pepper to taste and mix well. Spoon mixture over cheese-vegetable mixture, but do not stir.

- Cover and bake 35 minutes or until center of pie is firm. Remove from oven, sprinkle remaining cheese over top and return to oven for 5 minutes.

Chicken and Ham, Plus

2 cups cooked, cubed chicken or turkey	480 ml
2 cups cooked, cubed ham	480 ml
1 (8 ounce) package shredded cheddar cheese	227 g
1 (15 ounce) can English peas, drained	425 g
1 cup chopped onion	240 ml
1 cup chopped celery	240 ml
¼ cup (½ stick) butter	60 ml
⅓ cup flour	80 ml
1 pint half-and-half cream	.5 kg
⅛ teaspoon dry mustard	.5 ml
⅛ teaspoon nutmeg	.5 ml
Hot, cooked instant brown rice	

• In large bowl, combine chicken, ham, cheese and peas. In large saucepan, saute onion and celery in butter. Add flour and stir to make paste. Gradually add cream, mustard, nutmeg and salt and pepper to taste. Cook, stirring constantly, until mixture thickens. Add cream sauce to chicken-ham mixture and mix well.

• Spoon into buttered 3-quart (3 L) baking dish. Cover and bake for 20 minutes or until mixture is hot and bubbly. To serve, spoon chicken-ham mixture over hot cooked brown rice.

Old-Fashioned Turkey-Ham Bake

1 (8 ounce) package vermicelli, broken in small pieces	227 g
1 tablespoon oil	15 ml
1 (10 ounce) can cream of chicken soup	280 g
1 (10 ounce) can cream of mushroom soup	280 g
1 cup milk	240 ml
2 cups cooked, cubed turkey	480 ml
2 cups cooked, cubed ham	480 ml
1 red bell pepper, chopped	
1 green bell pepper, chopped	
1 (4 ounce) can sliced ripe olives	114 g
1 (12 ounce) package shredded processed cheese, divided	340 g

• Preheat oven to 350° (176° C). Cook vermicelli according to package directions. Drain and stir in oil and 1 teaspoon (5 ml) each of salt and pepper to keep vermicelli from sticking.

• In saucepan, combine both soups and milk and heat just enough to mix well. Stir in turkey, ham, bell peppers, ripe olives and half cheese.

• Spoon into buttered 9 x 13-inch (23 x 33 cm) baking dish.

• Cover and bake 35 minutes or until casserole is hot and bubbly. Remove from oven, sprinkle remaining cheese over top and return to oven for 5 minutes.

● ● ●

Rolled Chicken Florentine

6 boneless, skinless chicken breast halves	
6 thin slices deli ham	
6 thin slices Swiss cheese	
1 (10 ounce) package frozen chopped spinach, thawed, drained	280 g
2 (10 ounce) cans cream of chicken soup	2 (280 g)
4 fresh green onions, finely chopped	
⅛ teaspoon dried thyme	.5 ml
1 (10 ounce) box chicken-flavored Rice-a-Roni	280 g

• With flat side of meat mallet, pound chicken to ¼-inch (.6 cm) thickness. Place ham slice, cheese slice and one-eighth of well-drained spinach on each chicken piece. Roll chicken from short end, jellyroll fashion. Secure with wooden toothpicks if needed.

• Place chicken in buttered 9 x 13-inch (23 x 33 cm) baking dish. Cover with plastic wrap and microwave on HIGH for 5 minutes.

• Preheat oven to 325° (162° C). In bowl, stir together chicken soup, onions, thyme, ⅔ cup (160 ml) water and pepper to taste and blend well. Pour over chicken. Cover and bake for 20 minutes or until chicken is fork-tender.

• Cook Rice-a-Roni according to package directions*. Place on serving platter and spoon chicken and sauce over rice.

*Tip: You will need 3 tablespoons/45 ml butter.

Green Chili Chicken

1 (16 ounce) package frozen chopped onions and bell peppers	.5 kg
3 ribs celery, chopped	
1 (10 ounce) package frozen chopped spinach, thawed	280 g
1 (7 ounce) can green chilies	198 g
1 (8 ounce) carton sour cream	227 g
2 (10 ounce) cans cream of chicken soup	2 (280 g)
1 (13 ounce) package tortilla chips, slightly crushed	370 g
4 cups cooked, diced chicken or deli turkey	1 L
1 (8 ounce) package shredded Monterey Jack cheese	227 g

• Preheat oven to 350° (176° C). In skillet with little oil, saute onions and bell peppers and celery. Drain spinach well with several sheets of paper towels. Add spinach, green chilies, sour cream and both cans soup and mix well.

• In buttered 9 x 13-inch (23 x 33 cm) baking dish, place layer of crushed chips, half diced chicken, half spinach mixture and half cheese. Repeat layers with exception of cheese. Cover and bake 35 minutes. Remove from oven, sprinkle remaining cheese on top of casserole and return to oven for 5 minutes.

• • • • • • • • • •

Chicken With All The Extras

1 (6 ounce) box long grain and wild rice, cooked	168 g
1 pound pork sausage	.5 kg
2 cups chopped onion	480 ml
2 cups chopped celery	480 ml
2 sweet red bell peppers, chopped	
1 (7 ounce) can green chilies	198 g
4 boneless, skinless chicken breasts cooked, sliced	
3 tablespoons butter	45 ml
¼ cup flour	60 ml
1 cup heavy cream	240 ml
1 (14 ounce) can chicken broth	396 g
2½ cups buttery cracker crumbs	600 ml

• Preheat oven to 350° (176° C). Cook rice according to package directions. In large skillet, brown pork sausage and remove with slotted spoon. In same skillet, saute onion, celery and bell peppers. Drain and stir in green chilies and chicken slices.

• In saucepan, melt butter, stir in flour and mix well. On medium-high heat, stir in cream and chicken broth and stir constantly until mixture thickens.

• In large bowl, combine rice, sausage, vegetables, green chilies and chicken and mix thoroughly. Spoon into butter 9 x 13-inch (23 x 33 cm) baking dish. Sprinkle with cracker crumbs and bake 30 minutes.

● ● ●

• • • • • • • • • • •

Chicken-Broccoli Deluxe Supper

½ cup (1 stick) butter	120 ml
½ cup flour	120 ml
1 (10 ounce) can chicken broth	280 g
1 pint half-and-half cream	.5 kg
1 (12 ounce) package shredded cheddar cheese, divided	340 g
2 tablespoons lemon juice	30 ml
1 tablespoon prepared mustard	15 ml
¾ teaspoon dried basil	4 ml
⅔ cup mayonnaise	160 ml
1 (16 ounce) package frozen broccoli florets, thawed	.5 kg
4 large cooked, chicken breast halves, sliced	
1 (7 ounce) box vermicelli	198 g

• Preheat oven to 325° (162° C). Melt butter in large skillet. Add flour and mix well. Over low-medium heat, gradually add chicken broth and cream, stirring constantly, until it thickens. Add half cheese, lemon juice, mustard, basil and salt and pepper to taste. Stir in mayonnaise.

• Cook broccoli in microwave according to package directions. Gently add drained broccoli and chicken slices to sauce.

• Cook vermicelli according to package directions, drain and place in deep, greased 9 x 13-inch (23 x 33 cm) baking dish. Spoon chicken mixture over vermicelli. Cover and bake 35 minutes. Uncover, spread remaining cheese on top and return to oven for 5 minutes.

• • • • • • • • •

Garden Chicken

½ cup (1 stick) butter, divided	120 ml
4 boneless, skinless chicken breast halves, cut in strips	
1 teaspoon minced garlic	5 ml
1 zucchini, julienned	
1 yellow squash, julienned	
1 sweet red bell pepper, seeded, julienned	
4 tablespoons flour	60 ml
2 teaspoons pesto seasoning	10 ml
1 (14 ounce) can chicken broth	396 g
1 cup half-and-half cream	240 ml
1 (8 ounce) package angel hair pasta, cooked	227 g
⅓ cup shredded parmesan cheese	80 ml

• Preheat oven to 350° (176° C). In large skillet, with one-third of butter, cook chicken and garlic about 15 minutes over medium heat. Remove to warm plate and set aside. With half remaining butter, saute zucchini, squash and bell pepper until tender-crisp.

• In small saucepan melt remaining butter with flour, pesto and salt and pepper to taste. Stir to form smooth paste. Gradually add broth and cream, stirring constantly, until mixture thickens.

• In large bowl, combine chicken, vegetables, sauce mixture and drained pasta. Transfer to greased 9 x 13-inch (23 x 33 cm) baking dish. Cover and bake 30 minutes. Uncover and sprinkle parmesan over top and return to oven for 5 minutes.

● ● ●

Chicken Lasagna

1 (16 ounce) jar prepared alfredo sauce	.5 kg
1 (4 ounce) can sliced mushrooms, drained	114 g
1 (4 ounce) can diced pimentos, drained	114 g
⅓ cup dry white wine	80 ml
1 (10 ounce) box frozen chopped spinach, thawed	280 g
1 (15 ounce) carton ricotta cheese	425 g
½ cup grated parmesan cheese	120 ml
1 egg, beaten	
8 lasagna noodles	
3 cups cooked, chicken, shredded or deli turkey	710 ml
1 (12 ounce) package shredded cheddar cheese	340 g

• Preheat oven to 350° (176° C). In large bowl, combine alfredo sauce, mushrooms, pimentos and wine. Reserve ½ cup (120 ml) mixture for top of lasagna.

• Drain spinach well between several layers of paper towels. In another bowl, combine spinach, ricotta, parmesan and egg and mix well.

• Butter deep 9 x 13-inch (23 x 33 cm) baking dish and place 4 noodles in dish. Layer with half remaining sauce, half spinach-ricotta mixture and half chicken. (Spinach-ricotta mixture will be fairly dry so you will need to "spoon" it on and spread out.) Sprinkle with half cheese. For last layer, place noodles, remaining sauce, remaining spinach-ricotta mixture, chicken and reserved sauce.

• Cover and bake for 45 minutes. Sprinkle remaining cheese and return to oven for 5 minutes. Let casserole stand 10 minutes before serving.

Chinese-American Supper

1 (6 ounce) box Rice-a-Roni fried rice	168 g
1 cup chopped onion	240 ml
1 cup chopped celery	240 ml
1 (15 ounce) can Chinese vegetables, drained	425 g
1 (8 ounce) can sliced bamboo shoots	227 g
3 cups cooked, chopped chicken breast or turkey	710 ml
1 (10 ounce) can cream of chicken soup	280 g
1 cup mayonnaise	240 ml
2 tablespoons soy sauce	30 ml
1 cup chow mein noodles	240 ml

• Preheat oven to 350° (176° C). Cook rice according to package directions and set aside. In large skillet with little oil, saute, onion and celery, but do not brown. Add Chinese vegetables, bamboo shoots and chicken and mix well.

• In saucepan, heat chicken soup, mayonnaise, soy sauce and pepper to taste.

• In large bowl, combine rice, vegetable-chicken mixture and soup mixture, mix well and spoon into buttered 3-quart (3 L) baking dish.

• Sprinkle chow mein noodles over casserole and bake uncovered for 35 minutes.

Chicken and Different Dumpling

5 large boneless, skinless chicken breast halves	.5 kg
3 celery ribs, chopped	
1 onion, chopped	
1 bell pepper, seeded, chopped	
2 tablespoons dry chicken bouillon	30 ml
1 (10 ounce) can cream of chicken soup	280 g
10 (8-inch) flour tortillas, cut in (1-inch/2.5 cm) strips.	10 (20 cm)

• In large roasting pan, place chicken, 10 cups (2 L) water, celery, onion, bell pepper and generous amount of pepper. Bring to boil, reduce heat and cook for 30 minutes. Remove chicken and reserve broth in roaster. (You should have about 8 to 9 cups (2 L) broth remaining.) Let chicken cool and cut into bite-size pieces. Set aside.

• Return broth to boil and stir in chicken bouillon and chicken soup. Add strips, one at a time, to briskly boiling broth mixture and stir gently, but constantly. Reduce heat to medium while stirring in all remaining tortilla strips. Reduce heat to low, add chicken pieces and stir gently to prevent dumplings from sticking.

● ● ●

Chicken Supper Supreme

1 cup chopped onion	240 ml
1 cup chopped celery	240 ml
1 sweet red bell pepper, seeded, chopped	
4 cups cooked, cubed chicken or deli turkey	1 L
1 (6 ounce) box long grain and wild rice, cooked	168 g
1 (10 ounce) can cream of chicken soup	280 g
1 (15 ounce) can cut green beans, drained	425 g
1 cup slivered almonds	240 ml
1 cup mayonnaise	240 ml
2½ cups crushed potato chips	600 ml

- Preheat oven to 350° (176° C). In large skillet with little oil, saute onion, celery and bell pepper. Stir in chicken, rice, chicken soup, green beans, almonds, mayonnaise and 1 teaspoon (5 ml) each of salt and pepper. Gently mix until they blend.

- Spoon into greased 9 x 13-inch (23 x 33 cm) baking dish. Top with crushed potato chips and bake 35 minutes.

Confetti Squash and Chicken

1 pound yellow squash, sliced	.5 kg
1 pound zucchini, sliced	.5 kg
1 large onion, coarsely chopped	
2 carrots, grated	
2 cups cooked, cubed chicken or turkey	480 ml
1 (10 ounce) can cream of chicken soup	280 g
1 (8 ounce) carton sour cream	227 g
1 (4 ounce) can chopped pimento, drained	114 g
½ cup (1 stick) butter, melted	120 ml
1 (6 ounce) box herb stuffing mix	168 g

• Preheat oven to 350° (176° C). In large saucepan, cook squash, zucchini, onion and carrots in salted water for about 10 minutes. Drain and stir in chicken, soup, sour cream and pimentos and mix well.

• Combine melted butter and stuffing mix, add to vegetable-chicken mixture and mix well.

• Spoon into greased 9 x 13-inch (23 x 33 cm) baking dish. Cover and bake for 35 minutes.

Zesty Chicken and Spinach Bake

1 cup onion, chopped	240 ml
1 cup red bell pepper, chopped	240 ml
1 (10 ounce) package frozen spinach, cooked, drained	280 g
5 jalapenos, seeded, chopped or 1 (7 ounce) can green chilies	198 g
1 (8 ounce) carton sour cream	227 g
2 (10 ounce) cans cream of chicken soup	2 (280 g)
1 bunch fresh green onions, sliced	
1 (13 ounce) bag corn chips, slightly crushed	370 g
4 cups cooked, cubed chicken or turkey	1 L
1 (8 ounce) package shredded Monterey Jack cheese	227 g

• Preheat oven to 350° (176° C). In large skillet with little oil, saute onion and bell pepper. Blend in spinach, jalapenos, sour cream, chicken soup, green onions and salt and pepper to taste.

• Pour into buttered, deep 9 x 13-inch (23 x 33 cm) baking pan. Make layer of half chips, half chicken and half spinach mixture and top with half cheese. Repeat all layers except cheese.

• Cover and bake 35 minutes. Remove from oven, sprinkle remaining cheese over top and return to oven for 5 minutes.

Three-Cheesy Casserole

1 (8 ounce) package egg noodles	227 g
1 cup chopped onion	240 ml
1 cup chopped celery	240 ml
1 sweet red bell pepper, seeded, chopped	
1 (10 ounce) can cream of chicken soup	280 g
½ cup half-and-half cream	120 ml
1 (4 ounce) can sliced mushrooms	114 g
1 (12 ounce) carton small curd cottage cheese	340 g
4 cups cooked, diced turkey or chicken	1 L
1 (8 ounce) package shredded cheddar cheese	227 g
¾ cup grated parmesan cheese	180 ml

• Preheat oven to 350° (176° C). Cook noodles according to package directions. In skillet with little oil, saute onion, celery and bell pepper.

• In large bowl, combine onion, celery, bell pepper, soup, cream, mushrooms, cottage cheese, chicken, cheddar cheese and cooked, drained noodles. Toss with salt and pepper to taste.

• Pour into buttered 4-quart (4 L) baking dish and bake 35 minutes. Remove from oven, top with parmesan and return to oven for 5 minutes.

• • • • • • • • • • •

Sausage-Chicken-Mushroom Casserole

1 pound pork sausage	.5 kg
1 pound carton fresh mushrooms, sliced	.5 kg
2 onions, chopped	
3 cups cooked, cubed chicken or turkey	710 ml
¼ cup (½ stick) butter	60 ml
¼ cup flour	60 ml
1 (8 ounce) carton whipping cream	227 g
1 (14 ounce) can chicken broth	396 g
1 (6 ounce) box long grain and wild rice mix, cooked	168 g
2 cups buttery cracker crumbs	480 ml

• Preheat oven to 350° (176° C). In large skillet, brown and cook sausage, drain with slotted spoon and saute mushrooms and onions in same skillet. Drain and stir in chicken.

• Melt butter in saucepan. Add flour and mix. Over medium heat, add cream and broth and cook, stirring constantly, until mixture thickens. Transfer to large bowl and add rice, sausage and mushroom-chicken mixture. Mix until they blend well.

• Spoon into greased 9 x 13-inch (23 x 33 cm) baking dish. Sprinkle butter crumbs over top and bake 30 minutes.

● ● ●

• • • • • • • • • •

Asparagus-Cheese Chicken

1 tablespoon butter	15 ml
4 boneless, skinless chicken breast halves	
1 (10 ounce) can condensed broccoli-cheese soup	280 g
1 (10 ounce) package frozen asparagus cuts	280 g
1/3 cup milk	80 ml

• In skillet, heat butter and cook chicken 10 to 15 minutes or until brown on both sides. Remove chicken and set aside.

• In same skillet, combine soup, asparagus and milk and heat to boiling.

• Return chicken to skillet, reduce heat to low, cover and cook another 25 minutes until chicken is no longer pink and asparagus is tender.

• • •

Saucy Chicken

5 - 6 boneless, skinless chicken breast halves	
2 cups thick, chunky salsa	480 ml
1/3 cup packed light brown sugar	80 ml
1½ tablespoons dijon-style mustard	22 ml

• Place chicken breasts in greased 9 x 13-inch (23 x 33 cm) baking dish. Combine salsa, sugar and mustard and pour over chicken.

• Cover and bake at 350° (176° C) for 45 minutes. Serve over rice.

Mexican Fiesta

3 cups cooked, diced chicken or deli turkey	710 ml
1 onion, chopped	
1 (11 ounce) can mexicorn, drained	312 g
1 (12 ounce) package shredded, processed cheese	340 g
1 sweet red bell pepper, seeded, chopped	
1 teaspoon chili powder	5 ml
1 teaspoon cumin	5 ml
2 (10 ounce) cans cream of chicken soup	2 (280 g)
1 (15 ounce) can Mexican stewed tomatoes	425 g
1 (13 ounce) bag tortilla chips	370 g

- Preheat oven to 350° (176° C). In large bowl, combine chicken, onion, corn, cheese, bell pepper, chili powder, cumin, soup and tomatoes.

- Butter deep 9 x 13-inch (23 x 33 cm) baking pan, place about one-third to one-half tortilla chips in bottom of pan and crush slightly with palm of hand.

- Spoon chicken-soup mixture over chips and spread out. Crush some of remaining chips slightly (about 1 cup/240 ml) and spread over casserole. (You may need to use all chips.)

- Bake uncovered for 40 minutes.

Chicken-Spaghetti Bake

1 (10 ounce) package spaghetti	280 g
1 onion, chopped	
1 rib celery, chopped	
1 bell pepper, seeded, chopped	
1 (15 ounce) can Mexican stewed tomatoes	425 g
1 (4 ounce) can chopped mushrooms, drained	114 g
1 teaspoon minced garlic	5 ml
½ cup chicken broth	120 ml
4 cups cooked, cubed chicken	1 L
1 (12 ounce) package shredded processed cheese	340 g

• Preheat oven to 350° (176° C). Cook spaghetti according to package directions.

• In saucepan with little oil, saute onion, celery and bell pepper. Add tomatoes, mushrooms, garlic, broth, chicken and salt and pepper to taste.

• Stir in cheese and spoon into greased 4-quart (4 L) baking dish.

• Cover and bake 45 minutes.

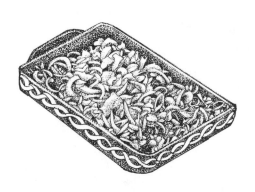

Extra Special Tetrazzini

1 (8 ounce) package thin spaghetti, cooked, drained	227 g
½ cup slivered almonds	120 ml
1 (10 ounce) can cream of mushroom soup	280 g
1 (10 ounce) can cream of chicken soup	280 g
1 cup half-and-half cream	240 ml
2 cups cooked, diced chicken or turkey	480 ml
2 cups cooked, diced ham	480 ml
1 sweet red bell pepper, seeded, chopped	
½ cup pitted ripe olives, halved	120 ml
1 (12 ounce) package shredded processed cheese, divided	340 g

- Preheat oven to 350° (176° C). Place cooked spaghetti in large bowl and add almonds, both soups, cream, chicken, ham, bell pepper, olives and salt and pepper to taste. Toss to mix well.

- Stir in half cheese and spoon into greased 9 x 13-inch (23 x 33 cm) baking pan. Cover and bake 35 minutes.

- Remove from oven and sprinkle remaining cheese over top of casserole and return to oven for 5 minutes.

Baked Turkey and Dressing

1 (6 ounce) package turkey dressing	168 g
3 cups diced, cooked turkey	710 ml
1 (15 ounce) can whole kernel corn	425 g
1 (4 ounce) can chopped green chilies, drained	114 g
1 sweet red bell pepper, seeded, chopped	
2 tablespoons dried parsley flakes	30 ml
1 (10 ounce) can cream of chicken soup	280 g
1 (8 ounce) carton sour cream	227 g
2 tablespoons (¼ stick) butter, melted	30 ml
1 teaspoon ground cumin	5 ml
1½ cups shredded mozzarella cheese	360 ml

• Preheat oven to 350° (176° C).

• In large mixing bowl, combine all ingredients except mozzarella cheese. Mix well and spoon into greased 9 x 13-inch (23 x 33 cm) baking dish.

• Cover and bake 35 minutes. Uncover and sprinkle with cheese and bake additional 5 minutes.

⬤ ⬤ ⬤

• • • • • • • • • •

Chicken Medley Supreme

1 cup chopped onion	240 ml
1 cup chopped celery	240 ml
3 cups cooked, diced chicken or turkey	710 ml
1 (6 ounce) package long grain and wild rice, cooked	168 g
1 (10 ounce) can cream of chicken soup	280 g
1 (4 ounce) jar chopped pimentos	114 g
1 (15 ounce) can French-style green beans, drained	425 g
½ cup slivered almonds	120 ml
1 cup mayonnaise	240 ml
3 cups lightly crushed potato chips	710 ml

• Preheat oven to 350° (176° C). In skillet with little oil, saute onion and celery. In large bowl, combine onion, celery, chicken, rice, chicken soup, pimentos, green beans, almonds, mayonnaise and salt and pepper to taste.

• Butter deep 9 x 13-inch (23 x 33 cm) baking dish and spoon mixture into dish. Sprinkle crushed potato chips over casserole and bake for 35 minutes or until chips are light brown.

● ● ●

Lemonade Chicken

6 boneless, skinless chicken breast halves
1 (6 ounce) can frozen lemonade, thawed   168 g
⅓ cup soy sauce   80 ml
1 teaspoon garlic powder   5 ml

• Place chicken in greased 9 x 13-inch (23 x 33 cm) baking dish.

• Combine lemonade, soy sauce and garlic powder and pour over chicken.

• Cover with foil and bake at 350° (176° C) for 45 minutes.

• Uncover, pour juices over chicken and cook another 10 minutes uncovered.

Sunday Chicken

5 - 6 boneless, skinless chicken breast halves
½ cup sour cream   120 ml
¼ cup soy sauce   60 ml
1 (10 ounce) can French onion soup   280 g

• Place chicken in greased 9 x 13-inch (23 x 33 cm) baking dish.

• In saucepan, combine sour cream, soy sauce and soup and heat just enough to mix well. Pour over chicken breasts.

• Bake covered at 350° (176° C) for 55 minutes.

Beef
Entrees

Chili Relleno Casserole

1 pound lean ground beef	.5 kg
1 onion, chopped	
1 bell pepper, chopped	
1 teaspoon oregano	5 ml
1 teaspoon minced garlic	5 ml
1 cup whole green chilies	240 ml
1 (12 ounce) package shredded Monterey	
Jack cheese	340 g
3 large eggs, beaten	
1 cup half-and-half cream	240 ml

- Preheat oven to 350° (176° C). In skillet with little oil, brown beef, onion, bell pepper and salt and pepper to taste. Stir in oregano and garlic.

- Spread green chilies in bottom of greased 9 x 13-inch (23 x 33 cm) baking dish. Cover with meat-onion mixture and sprinkle with cheese.

- Combine beaten eggs and cream and pour over top of meat mixture. Bake uncovered for 35 minutes or until top is slightly brown.

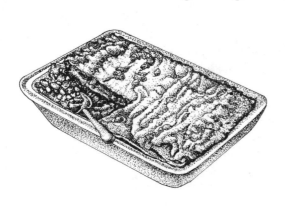

• • • • • • • • • • •

Cheeseburger Pie

1 pound lean ground beef	.5 kg
1 onion, chopped	
1 cup chili sauce	240 ml
1 (10-inch/25 cm) deep-dish piecrust	
1 egg, beaten	
1 teaspoon Worcestershire sauce	5 ml
¼ cup milk	60 ml
1 (8 ounce) package shredded American cheese	227 g

• Preheat oven to 350° (176° C). In large skillet with little oil, brown beef, onion and salt and pepper to taste. Drain. Stir in chili sauce and simmer for 5 minutes. Pour into piecrust.

• For cheese topping, combine egg, Worcestershire, milk and cheese and mix well. Spoon over meat mixture and cook 30 minutes or until center of cheese layer is firm.

● ● ●

Cheesy Beefy Gnocchi

1 pound lean ground beef	.5 kg
1 (10 ounce) can cheddar cheese soup	280 g
1 (10 ounce) can tomato-bisque soup	280 g
2 cups uncooked gnocchi or shell pasta	480 ml

• In skillet, cook beef until brown and drain. Add soups, 1½ (360 ml) cups water and pasta. Bring mixture to boil. Cover and cook over medium heat for 10 to 12 minutes or until pasta is done and stir often.

Supper's Ready Quick

1 pound lean ground beef	.5 kg
1 onion, chopped	
2/3 cup chili sauce	160 ml
1 (15 ounce) can baked beans with liquid	425 g
1 (11 ounce) can mexicorn	312 g
2 cups crushed garlic-flavored croutons	480 ml

• Preheat oven to 350° (176° C). In skillet, brown beef, onion and salt and pepper to taste. Stir in chili sauce and simmer covered, on medium heat for 10 minutes.

• Stir in beans and corn and spoon into greased 3-quart (3 L) baking dish. Cover with croutons and bake 30 minutes.

Round Steak Casserole Supper

1½ pounds lean round steak, tenderized	.7 kg
1 onion, chopped	
1 green bell pepper, seeded, julienned	
1 red bell pepper, seeded, julienned	
1½ cups rice	360 ml
2 (10 ounce) cans beef broth	2 (280 g)
1 (7 ounce) can green chilies	198 g

• Trim edges of steak and cut into serving-size pieces.

• In large skillet with little oil, brown each piece of steak on both sides. Add onion, bell peppers, rice, beef broth and green chilies. Bring to boil. Reduce heat and simmer for 50 minutes.

Classic Beefy Noodles

1½ pounds lean ground beef	.7 kg
2 (10 ounce) cans tomatoes and green chilies	2 (280 g)
2 teaspoons minced garlic	10 ml
1 (8 ounce) package noodles	227 g
1 (3 ounce) package cream cheese	84 g
1 (8 ounce) carton sour cream	227 g
1 (8 ounce) package shredded cheddar cheese	227 g

• Preheat oven to 350° (176° C). In large skillet, brown beef. Drain and stir in tomatoes and green chilies, garlic and salt and pepper to taste. Bring to boil, reduce heat and simmer 25 minutes.

• While beef mixture cooks, place noodles in large saucepan and cook according to package directions. Drain, stir in cream cheese and stir until cream cheese melts. Fold in sour cream and stir in beef mixture.

• Spoon into greased 9 x 13-inch (23 x 33 cm) baking dish. Cover and bake 30 minutes. Remove from oven, sprinkle cheese over top and return to oven for 5 minutes.

Supper Casserole

1 pound lean ground beef	.5 kg
1 cup onion, chopped	240 ml
1 cup bell pepper, chopped	240 ml
2 (10 ounce) cans golden mushroom soup	2 (280 g)
⅔ cup uncooked rice	160 ml
3 tablespoons soy sauce	45 ml
1 (8 ounce) can green peas	227 g
1 (3 ounce) can french-fried onions	84 g

- Preheat oven to 350° (176° C). In large skillet, brown ground beef. Drain. Add onion, bell pepper, soup, rice, soy sauce, peas and 2 cups (480 ml) water and mix well.

- Spoon into greased 9 x 13-inch (23 x 33 cm) baking dish. Cover and bake 50 minutes. Remove from oven, sprinkle fried onions over casserole and return to oven for 10 minutes.

Chihuahua Dogs

1 (10 ounce) can chili hot dog sauce	280 g
1 (10 count) package frankfurters	
10 pre-formed taco shells	
Shredded cheddar cheese	

- Place hot dog sauce in saucepan.

- Place frank in each taco shell. Top with heated chili sauce and cheese. (Onions and tomatoes optional.)

- Place in microwave and heat for 30 seconds or until frankfurters warm.

Corned Beef Supper

3 - 4 pounds corned beef brisket   **1.3 kg**
4 medium potatoes, peeled, quartered
6 carrots, peeled, quartered
1 medium head cabbage

• Place corned beef in roasting pan, cover with water and bring to boil. Reduce heat and simmer for 3 hours.

• Add potatoes and carrots. Add more water if necessary.

• Cut cabbage into eighths and lay over top of potatoes and carrots. Bring to boil, reduce heat and cook 30 to 40 minutes or until vegetables are tender.

• Place brisket on serving platter and slice across grain. Serve with vegetables.

• • • • • • • • • • •

Sauerkraut and Hot Dog Supper

1 (27 ounce) can sauerkraut, rinsed, drained   750 g
2 teaspoons caraway seeds   10 ml
8 beef hot dogs, halved lengthwise
1½ cups shredded Swiss cheese   360 ml
Thousand Island salad dressing, optional
Cornbread muffins

- Preheat oven to 350° (176° C). Place sauerkraut in greased 7 x 11-inch (18 x 28 cm) baking dish and sprinkle with caraway seeds. Place hot dogs on top.

- Bake uncovered for 20 minutes or until thoroughly hot. Sprinkle cheese on top and bake another 5 minutes. Serve with salad dressing.

- To make cornbread, use 1 (8 ounce/227 g) package cornbread mix, 1 egg and ⅓ cup (80 ml) milk and bake according to package directions.

● ● ●

Shepherd's Pie

1 pound lean ground beef	.5 kg
1 (1.25 ounce) envelope taco seasoning mix	38 g
1 cup shredded cheddar cheese	240 ml
1 (11 ounce) can mexicorn	312 g
1 (20 ounce) package frozen mashed potatoes, thawed	567 g

• Preheat oven to 350° (176° C). In skillet, brown beef and cook 10 minutes, drain. Add taco seasoning and ½ cup (120 ml) water and cook another 10 minutes.

• Spoon beef mixture into greased 9-inch (23 cm) baking pan. Sprinkle cheese on top, then corn. Spread mashed potatoes over top. Bake uncovered for 25 to 30 minutes or until top is golden.

Bueno Taco Casserole

2 pounds ground beef	1 kg
1½ cups taco sauce	360 ml
2 (15 ounce) cans Spanish rice	2 (425 g)
1 (8 ounce) package shredded Mexican 4-cheese blend, divided	227 g

• In skillet, brown ground beef and drain. Add taco sauce, Spanish rice and half cheese. Spoon into buttered 3-quart (3 L) baking dish.

• Cover and bake at 350° (176° C) for 35 minutes. Uncover and sprinkle remaining cheese on top and return to oven for 5 minutes.

• • • • • • • • • • •

Beefy Potato Bake

1½ pounds lean ground beef	.7 kg
1 onion, chopped	
4 medium potatoes, peeled, sliced	
1 (10 ounce) can golden mushroom soup	280 g
1 (10 ounce) can condensed vegetable-beef soup	280 g
1 (3 ounce) can french-fried onion rings	84 g

• Preheat oven to 350° (176° C). In skillet, brown and cook beef and onion 10 minutes. In large bowl, combine beef mixture, sliced potatoes and both soups and mix well.

• Transfer to greased 3-quart (3 L) baking dish. Cover and bake 1 hour 10 minutes. Uncover and spread onion rings over top of casserole and return to oven for 15 minutes.

• • •

Quick Chili Casserole

1 (40 ounce) can chili with beans	1.1 kg
1 (4 ounce) can chopped green chilies	114 g
1 (11 ounce) can mexicorn	312 g
1 (2 ounce) can sliced ripe olives	57 g
1 (8 ounce) package shredded cheddar cheese	227 g
2 cups crushed, ranch-flavored tortilla chips	480 ml

• Preheat oven to 350° (176° C). In large bowl, combine all ingredients and mix well.

• Transfer to greased 3-quart (3 L) baking dish. Bake uncovered for 35 minutes or until bubbly.

• • • • • • • • • • •

Savory Beef and Bean Pie

1 pound lean ground beef	.5 kg
1 onion, chopped	
3 ribs celery, sliced	
2 (15 ounce) cans pinto beans, drained	2 (425 g)
2 (10 ounce) cans tomatoes and green chilies	2 (280 g)
1½ cups crushed tortilla chips	360 ml
1 (3 ounce) can french-fried onion rings	84 g

• Preheat oven to 350° (176° C). In skillet, brown beef, onion and celery. Drain.

• In greased 3-quart (3 L) baking dish, layer 1 can beans, beef-onion mixture and 1 can tomatoes and green chilies. Repeat layers and sprinkle tortilla chips over top.

• Bake 20 minutes, remove from oven and spread onion rings over chips and return to oven for 15 minutes.

● ● ●

Asian Beef and Noodles

1½ pounds lean ground beef	.7 kg
2 (3 ounce) packages Oriental-flavored ramen noodles	2 (84 g)
1 (16 ounce) frozen Oriental stir-fry vegetables, thawed	.5 kg
½ teaspoon ground ginger	2 ml
1 bunch fresh green onions, sliced	

• In large skillet, cook ground beef and drain. Add ½ cup (120 ml) water and simmer 10 minutes. Transfer to separate bowl.

• In same skillet, combine 2 cups (480 ml) water, broken up noodles, vegetables, ginger and both seasoning packets from ramen noodles. Bring to boil, reduce heat, cover and simmer 3 minutes, stirring occasionally.

• Return beef to skillet and stir in green onions. Serve right from skillet.

• • • • • • • • • • •

Spicy Beef and Noodles

1 pound lean ground beef	.5 kg
1 (1.25 ounce) package taco seasoning mix	38 g
1 (15 ounce) can Mexican stewed tomatoes	425 g
1 (15 ounce) can pinto beans with liquid	425 g
1 pound package egg noodles	.5 kg
1 bunch fresh green onions, sliced	

• Cook beef in large skillet and drain. Add taco seasoning with ½ cup (120 ml) water and simmer 15 minutes.

• Stir in stewed tomatoes, pinto beans and salt and pepper to taste.

• Cook noodles according to package directions and place on serving platter. Spoon spicy beef over noodles and sprinkle with sliced green onions.

• • •

Slow Cookin', Good Tastin' Brisket

½ cup liquid hickory-flavored smoke	120 ml
1 (4 - 5 pound) beef brisket	2.2 kg
1 (5 ounce) bottle Worcestershire sauce	143 g
¾ cup barbecue sauce	180 ml

• Pour liquid smoke over brisket. Cover and refrigerate overnight. Drain and pour Worcestershire sauce over brisket.

• Cover and bake at 275° (135° C) for 6 to 7 hours. Cover with barbecue sauce. Bake uncovered for another 30 minutes. Slice very thin across grain.

Oriental Beef and Noodles

1 pound lean ground beef	.5 kg
2 (3 ounce) packages Oriental ramen noodles, crumbled	2 (84 g)
1 (16 ounce) package frozen broccoli stir-fry vegetables	.5 kg
1 (10 ounce) box frozen green peas, thawed	280 g
¼ teaspoon ground ginger	1 ml
3 fresh green onions, thinly sliced	

• In large skillet over medium heat, cook beef 6 minutes or until no longer pink. Stir in 1 flavoring packet from ramen noodles and mix well. Transfer to warm plate.

• In same skillet, combine stir-fry vegetables, peas, ginger, noodles, 2⅔ cups (640 ml) water and remaining flavoring packet. Bring to boil. Reduce heat, cover and simmer 5 minutes, stirring occasionally.

• Return beef to skillet and cook another 3 minutes or until thoroughly hot. Just before serving, stir in sliced onions.

Spaghetti Pie Special

6 ounces spaghetti, cooked, drained	168 g
⅓ cup grated parmesan cheese	80 ml
1 egg, beaten	
1 cup small curd cottage cheese, drained	240 ml
1 pound lean ground beef	.5 kg
½ cup chopped onion	120 ml
1 (15 ounce) can tomato sauce	425 g
1 teaspoon minced garlic	5 ml
1 teaspoon dried oregano	5 ml
1 tablespoon sugar	15 ml
½ cup mozzarella cheese	120 ml

- Preheat oven to 350° (176° C). Mix spaghetti while still warm with parmesan and egg in large bowl.

- Spoon onto well greased 10-inch (25 cm) pie plate (or pizza pan) and pat mixture up and around sides with spoon to form crust. Spoon cottage cheese over spaghetti layer.

- In skillet, brown meat and onion. Drain and add tomato sauce, seasonings and salt and pepper to taste. Simmer for 15 minutes.

- Spoon meat mixture over cottage cheese and bake 30 minutes. Sprinkle mozzarella on top and return to oven for 5 minutes or just until cheese melts. To serve, cut into wedges.

Taco Pie

1 pound lean ground beef	.5 kg
1 (11 ounce) can mexicorn, drained	312 g
1 (8 ounce) can tomato sauce	227 g
1 (1.25 ounce) envelope taco seasoning	38 g
1 (9-inch) frozen piecrust	23 cm
1 cup shredded cheddar cheese	240 ml

• Preheat oven to 350° (176° C). In large skillet, brown and cook ground beef until no longer pink. Stir in corn, tomato sauce and taco seasoning. Keep warm.

• Place piecrust in pie pan and bake 5 minutes. Remove from oven, spoon ground beef mixture onto piecrust and spread evenly.

• Sprinkle cheese over top and bake another 20 minutes or until filling bubbles.

• Let stand 5 minutes before slicing to serve.

• • • • • • • • • • •

Smothered Beef Patties

1½ pounds ground beef	680 g
½ cup chili sauce	120 ml
½ cup buttery cracker crumbs	120 ml
1 (14 ounce) can beef bouillon	396 g

• Combine beef, chili sauce and cracker crumbs and form into 5 or 6 patties. In skillet, brown patties and pour beef bouillon over patties.

• Bring to boil. Reduce heat and cover and simmer for about 40 minutes.

• • •

Mexican Casserole

1 (13 ounce) bag tortilla chips, divided	370 g
2 pounds lean ground beef	1 kg
1 (10 ounce) can Mexican stewed tomatoes	280 g
1 (8 ounce) package shredded Mexican 4-cheese blend	227 g

• Partially crush half bag chips and place in bottom of buttered 9 x 13-inch (23 x 33 cm) baking dish.

• Brown ground beef and drain.

• Add stewed tomatoes and cheese and mix well. Sprinkle finely crushed chips over casserole.

• Bake uncovered at 350° (176° C) for 40 minutes.

• • •

• • • • • • • • • •

Easy Breezy Brisket

1 (4 - 5 pound) brisket	2.2 kg
1 (1 ounce) package dry onion soup mix	28 g
2 tablespoons Worcestershire sauce	30 ml
1 cup red wine	240 ml

• Place brisket in shallow baking pan. Sprinkle onion soup over brisket.

• Pour Worcestershire and red wine in pan.

• Cover and bake at 325° (162° C) for 5 to 6 hours.

• • •

Next-Day Brisket

1 (5 - 6 pound) trimmed beef brisket	2.7 kg
1 (1 ounce) package dry onion soup mix	28 g
1 (10 ounce) bottle steak sauce	280 g
1 (12 ounce) bottle barbecue sauce	340 g

• Place brisket, cut side up, in roasting pan.

• In bowl, combine onion soup mix, steak sauce and barbecue sauce. Pour over brisket.

• Cover and cook at 325° (162° C) for 4 to 5 hours or until tender. Remove brisket from pan and pour off drippings. Chill both, separately, overnight.

• The next day, trim all fat from meat, slice and reheat. Skim fat off drippings and reheat. Serve sauce over brisket.

Pork
Main
Dishes

Baked Ham-and-Potato Supper

1 (24 ounce) package frozen hash browns with onions and peppers, thawed	680 g
3 cups cooked, cubed ham	710 ml
1 (10 ounce) can cream of chicken soup	280 g
1 (10 ounce) can cream of celery soup	280 g
1 (10 ounce) package frozen green peas, thawed	280 g
1 (8 ounce) package shredded Swiss cheese	227 g

• Preheat oven to 350° (176° C). In large bowl, combine hash browns, ham, both soups and peas and mix well.

• Spoon into greased 9 x 13-inch (23 x 33 cm) baking dish and bake 40 minutes. Remove from oven, uncover, sprinkle cheese over casserole and return to oven for another 5 minutes.

Baked Pork Chops

¾ cup ketchup	180 ml
¾ cup packed brown sugar	180 ml
¼ cup lemon juice	60 ml
4 butter-flied pork chops	

• Combine ketchup, ½ cup (120 ml) water, brown sugar and lemon juice.

• Place pork chops in 7 x 11-inch (18 x 28 cm) buttered baking dish and pour sauce over pork chops. Bake covered at 325° (162° C) for 50 minutes.

Ham and Wild Rice Bake

1 (6 ounce) box long grain and wild rice mix	168 g
1 (10 ounce) package frozen broccoli florets, thawed	280 g
1 (11 ounce) can mexicorn	312 g
3 cups cooked, cubed ham	710 ml
1 (10 ounce) can cream of mushroom soup	280 g
1 cup mayonnaise	240 ml
1 cup shredded cheddar cheese	240 ml
1 (3 ounce) can french-fried onion rings	84 g

- Preheat oven to 350° (176° C). Cook rice according to package directions and spread into greased 3-quart (3 L) baking dish. Top with broccoli, corn and ham.

- In large bowl, combine soup, mayonnaise, cheese and salt to taste. Spread over broccoli-ham mixture.

- Cover and bake 25 minutes. Remove from oven and sprinkle fried onions on top. Return to oven and bake another 15 minutes.

• • • • • • • • • • •

Fiesta Baked Potato

4 large baking potatoes
1 (10 ounce) can fiesta nacho cheese soup   280 g
1 cup shredded Mexican 3-cheese blend   240 ml
1 cup cooked, shredded ham   240 ml
¼ cup sour cream   60 ml
1 (10 ounce) package frozen broccoli florets,
    thawed   280 g

• Cook potatoes in microwave until tender. In 1-quart (1 L) microwave-safe bowl, stir together soup, cheese, ham, sour cream, broccoli and salt and pepper to taste. Heat in microwave 2 to 3 minutes or until hot and bubbly.

• Spoon cheese mixture over split and fluffed up potatoes.

● ● ●

Ham and Sweet Potatoes

3 tablespoons dijon-style mustard, divided   45 ml
1 (3 - 4 pounds) boneless smoked ham   1.3 kg
½ cup honey or packed brown sugar   120 ml
1 (29 ounce) can sweet potatoes, drained   805 g

• Preheat oven to 325° (162° C).

• Spread mustard on ham. Place ham in prepared, shallow baking pan and bake for 20 minutes.

• Combine remaining mustard with brown sugar or honey and spread over ham. Add sweet potatoes, baste with sauce and bake for 20 minutes.

• • • • • • • • • • •

Ham-Stuffed Tomatoes

6 large tomatoes	
1 (10 ounce) package frozen chopped broccoli	280 g
1½ cups cooked, shredded ham	360 ml
1 (8 ounce) package shredded Mexican 3-cheese blend	227 g

• Preheat oven to 375° (190° C). Cut tops off tomatoes and scoop out pulp. Cook broccoli according to package directions. Drain.

• In bowl, combine broccoli, ham, 1 teaspoon (5 ml) salt and about three-fourths of cheese.

• Stuff broccoli mixture into tomatoes, place on baking sheet and bake 10 minutes. When serving, sprinkle remaining cheese over tops of stuffed tomatoes.

● ● ●

Eggs and Biscuit Supper

12 - 14 eggs, slightly beaten	
1 pound sausage, cooked, crumbled	.5 kg
2 cups milk	480 ml
1 (8 ounce) package shredded cheddar cheese	227 g
1 (5.5 ounce) box seasoned croutons	155 g
Hot biscuits	

• Preheat oven to 350° (176° C). In large bowl, combine all ingredients and pour into greased 9 x 13-inch (23 x 33 cm) baking dish.

• Cover and bake for 45 minutes or until center is firm. Let stand about 10 minutes before slicing to serve.

• When serving, cook 1 (22 ounce/624 g) package frozen buttermilk biscuits.

Colorful Sausage Supper

1 pound cooked Polish sausage, cut into (¼-inch/. 6 cm) slices	.5 kg
1 sweet red bell pepper, julienned	
3 small zucchini, sliced	
3 small yellow squash, sliced	
4 tablespoons olive oil, divided	60 ml
1 (16 ounce) package penne pasta	.5 kg
1 (26 ounce) jar spaghetti sauce, heated	737 g

• Saute sausage, bell pepper, zucchini and squash until vegetables are tender-crisp in large skillet with 2 tablespoons (30 ml) oil. Keep warm.

• Cook pasta according to package directions, drain and stir in remaining oil. Add salt and pepper to taste.

• Spoon into large serving bowl and spread hot spaghetti sauce over pasta.

• Use slotted spoon to top with sausage-vegetable mixture and serve immediately. Serve with hot, buttered garlic bread.

• • • • • • • • • •

Fiesta Corn and Ham

1 (15 ounce) can cream-style corn	425 g
1 (15 ounce) can whole kernel corn	425 g
1 bell pepper, chopped	
1 onion, chopped	
1 (4 ounce) can chopped green chilies	114 g
2 cups cooked, cubed ham*	480 ml
2 tablespoons (¼ stick) butter, melted	30 ml
2 large eggs, beaten	
1 tablespoon sugar	15 ml
½ cup buttery cracker crumbs	120 ml
1 cup shredded cheddar cheese	240 ml

Topping:
1 cup buttery cracker crumbs	240 ml
2 tablespoons shredded parmesan cheese	30 ml

• Preheat oven to 350° (176° C). In large bowl, combine both cans corn, bell pepper, onion, green chilies and ham and mix well. Stir in melted butter, eggs, sugar, cracker crumbs, cheese and salt and pepper to taste.

• Spoon into greased 9 x 13-inch (23 x 33 cm) baking dish and bake uncovered 30 minutes.

• Remove from oven, sprinkle cracker crumbs and parmesan over top of casserole and bake another 15 minutes.

*Tip: This is a good recipe for leftover ham or ham from the deli.

● ● ●

Ham, Noodles and the Works

1 (8 ounce) package small egg noodles	227 g
2 (10 ounce) cans cream of broccoli soup	2 (280 g)
1 (8 ounce) carton whipping cream	227 g
1 (8 ounce) can whole kernel corn, drained	227 g
1 (16 ounce) package frozen broccoli, cauliflower and carrots, thawed	.5 kg
3 cups cooked, cubed ham	710 ml
1 (8 ounce) package shredded cheddar-jack cheese, divided	227 g

• Preheat oven to 325° (162° C). Cook noodles according to package directions.

• In large bowl, combine broccoli soup, cream, corn, broccoli-carrot mixture, ham and salt and pepper to taste. Fold in noodles and half of cheese.

• Spoon into sprayed 9 x 13-inch (23 x 33 cm) baking dish. Cover and bake for 45 minutes. Remove from oven, sprinkle remaining cheese over top and return to oven for 5 minutes.

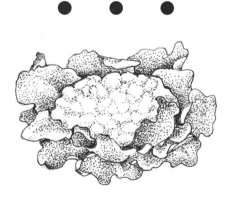

Savory Pork Chop Bake

8 lean pork chops	
1 onion, chopped	
1 red bell pepper, chopped	
1 (10 ounce) can cream of mushroom soup	280 g
1 cup uncooked rice	240 ml
1 cup shredded processed cheese	240 ml
1 (8 ounce) can green peas, drained	227 g
1 (4 ounce) can sliced mushrooms, drained	114 g
1 (3 ounce) can french-fried onions	84 g

• Preheat oven to 325° (162° C). Brown pork chops in large skillet with a little oil. Add onion and bell pepper and cook 10 minutes. Drain and place in greased 9 x 13-inch (23 x 33 cm) baking dish.

• In same skillet, combine mushroom soup, rice, cheese, green peas, mushrooms and 1¼ cups (300 ml) water and mix well.

• Spoon mixture over pork chops, onion and bell pepper. Cover and bake 50 minutes. Uncover and top with french-fried onions and cook another 15 minutes or until fried onions are light brown.

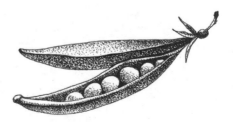

Supper Frittata

2 cups cooked white rice	480 ml
1 (10 ounce) box frozen green peas, thawed	280 g
1 cup cooked, cubed ham	240 ml
8 large eggs, beaten	
1 cup shredded pepper-jack cheese, divided	240 ml
1 teaspoon dried thyme	5 ml
1 teaspoon sage	5 ml

• Cook rice, peas and ham 3 to 4 minutes or until mixture is thoroughly hot in large heavy ovenproof skillet with a little oil.

• In separate bowl, whisk eggs, three-fourths of cheese, thyme, sage and 1 teaspoon (5 ml) salt. Add to mixture in skillet and shake pan gently to distribute evenly. On medium heat, cover and cook, without stirring, until set on bottom and sides. (Eggs will still be runny in center.)

• Sprinkle remaining cheese over top. Place skillet in oven and broil about 5 minutes or until frittata is firm in center.

● ● ●

Tasty Noodles and Pork

1½ pounds pork tenderloin, cubed	.7 kg
2 cups chopped celery	480 ml
2 cups chopped onion	480 ml
1 green bell pepper, chopped	
1 red bell pepper, chopped	
1 (14 ounce) can Mexican stewed tomatoes	396 g
2 (10 ounce) cans golden mushroom soup	2 (280 g)
¼ cup soy sauce	60 ml
1½ cups elbow macaroni, cooked, drained	360 ml
2 cups chow mein noodles	480 ml

- Preheat oven to 350° (176° C). In skillet with little oil, brown pork and cook on low heat for 15 minutes. Transfer pork with slotted spoon to side dish.

- In same skillet, saute celery, onion and bell peppers.

- In large bowl, combine pork, celery-pepper mixture, stewed tomatoes, mushroom soup, soy sauce and macaroni.

- Spoon into buttered 9 x 13-inch (23 x 33 cm) baking dish. Sprinkle chow mein noodles on top of casserole and bake 40 minutes.

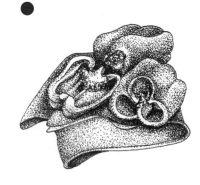

• • • • • • • • • • •

Zesty Pork Casserole

2 pounds boneless pork tenderloin, cubed	1 kg
1 green bell pepper, chopped	
1 red bell pepper, chopped	
2 teaspoons minced garlic	10 ml
1 (10 ounce) can fiesta nacho cheese soup	280 g
2 (15 ounce) cans black beans, rinsed, drained	2 (425 g)
2 (15 ounce) cans Mexican stewed tomatoes	2 (425 g)
1 cup instant brown rice, cooked	240 ml
¾ cup salsa	180 ml
2 teaspoons ground cumin	10 ml
1½ cups crushed tortilla chips	360 ml

• Preheat oven to 350° (176° C). In very large skillet with little oil, brown and cook pork, peppers and garlic until pork is no longer pink. Drain.

• Stir in nacho cheese, beans, stewed tomatoes, rice, salsa and cumin and mix well. Cook on medium heat, stirring occasionally, until mixture bubbles.

• Spoon into buttered 4-quart (4 L) baking dish, cover and bake 20 minutes. Remove from oven, sprinkle with tortilla chips and continue baking another 20 minutes or until tortilla chips are light brown.

• • •

Colorful Stir-Fried Pork & Vegetables

½ cup stir-fry sauce	120 ml
1 teaspoon white vinegar	5 ml
¼ teaspoon cayenne pepper	1 ml
3 tablespoons oil	45 ml
1 pound lean pork, cut in thin strips	.5 kg
3 medium carrots, julienned	
½ pound fresh snow peas, trimmed	227 g
1 sweet red bell pepper, seeded, julienned	
Hot, buttered rice	

• Combine stir-fry sauce, vinegar, cayenne pepper and salt to taste. Place oil in skillet on medium-high heat. Stir in sauce mixture and pork strips and toss to coat strips with sauce.

• Stir-fry 3 minutes and transfer to warm plate. In same skillet, stir-fry carrots, peas and bell pepper 5 minutes.

• Stir in pork; mix well and cook just until pork and sauce coats and vegetables are tender. Serve with hot, buttered rice.

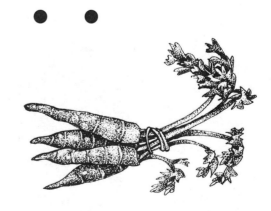

Ham Quesadillas

2 cups shredded ham	480 ml
½ cup chunky salsa	120 ml
2 teaspoons chili powder	10 ml
¾ cup whole kernel corn	180 ml
8 large whole-wheat tortillas	
1 (8 ounce) package shredded Mexican	
4-cheese blend	227 g

• In large bowl, combine shredded ham, salsa, chili powder and corn. Spread mixture over 4 tortillas to within ½-inch (1.2 cm) of edge. Then sprinkle cheese on top.

• Top with remaining tortillas and cook (1 quesadilla at a time) on medium-high heat, in large non-stick skillet about 5 minutes. Turn after 2 minutes or until light golden brown.

• Cut in wedges to serve and serve with pinto beans and guacamole.

Pork and Veggie Stir-Fry

1 (12 ounce) whole pork tenderloin, thinly sliced	340 g
2 tablespoons, peeled, grated fresh ginger	30 ml
1 (10 ounce) package frozen snow peas	280 g
2 small zucchini, halved lengthwise, sliced	
1 bunch green onions, cut in (3-inch/8 cm) pieces	
1 (10 ounce) can chicken broth	280 g
2 tablespoons teriyaki sauce	30 ml
1 tablespoon cornstarch	15 ml

• Stir-fry pork slices and ginger in large skillet with a little oil over medium-high heat, just until pork loses its pink color. Transfer to serving bowl and keep warm.

• In same skillet with little more oil, cook snow peas, zucchini and onions until tender-crisp.

• In small bowl, combine broth, teriyaki sauce and cornstarch and mix well. Pour into skillet with vegetables and heat to boiling. Boil, stirring constantly, until sauce thickens. Return pork to skillet, stir to coat with sauce and heat thoroughly.

• Serve with hot, buttered Italian bread.

Stove-Top Ham Supper

1 (12 ounce) package spiral pasta	340 g
3 tablespoons butter, sliced	45 ml
2 - 3 cups cooked, cubed ham	480 ml
1 teaspoon minced garlic	5 ml
1 (16 ounce) package frozen broccoli,	
cauliflower and carrots	.5 kg
½ cup sour cream	120 ml
1 (8 ounce) package shredded cheddar	
cheese, divided	227 g

• Preheat oven to 375° (190° C). Cook pasta in large saucepan, according to package directions. Drain. While still hot, stir in butter. Add ham, garlic and 1 teaspoon (5 ml) salt.

• Cook vegetables in microwave according to package directions and stir, undrained into pasta-ham mixture. Stir in sour cream and half cheese and mix until they blend well.

• Spoon into sprayed 3-quart (3 L) baking dish. Bake 15 minutes or just until bubbly around edges. Sprinkle remaining cheese on top and let stand just until cheese melts.

Sweet-and-Sour Pork Chop Bake

6 center-cut pork chops	
½ cup lemon juice	120 ml
4 tablespoons cornstarch	60 ml
¾ cup packed brown sugar	180 ml
1 tablespoon soy sauce	15 ml
1 (10 ounce) can chicken broth	280 g
1 (20 ounce) can pineapple chunks with juice	567 g
1 cup thinly sliced carrots	240 ml
Green pepper rings	
1 (6 ounce) box Roasted Garlic Long Grain and Wild Rice mix	168 g

• Preheat oven to 350° (176° C). In large skillet with little oil, brown pork chops and transfer to greased 9 x 13-inch (23 x 33 cm) baking dish.

• In same skillet combine lemon juice, cornstarch, brown sugar, soy sauce, chicken broth and about ½ cup (120 ml) pineapple juice and mix well. On medium heat, cook, stirring constantly, until mixture thickens.

• Pour mixture over pork chops and add carrots. Cover and bake 55 minutes. Uncover, add pineapple chunks and green pepper rings and cook another 10 minutes.

• Cook rice mix according to package directions and serve pork chops and sauce over rice.

Tenderloin, Noodles and Peas

1½ pounds pork tenderloin, cubed	.7 kg
1 cup chopped onion	240 ml
1 cup chopped celery	240 ml
2 sweet red bell peppers, seeded, chopped	
1 (8 ounce) package small egg noodles, cooked	227 g
1 (10 ounce) can cream of chicken soup	280 g
½ cup heavy cream	120 ml
1 (10 ounce) package frozen green peas, thawed	280 g
1½ cups seasoned breadcrumbs	360 ml
½ cup chopped walnuts	120 ml

• Preheat oven to 350° (176° C). In large skillet with little oil, brown pork tenderloin. Reduce heat and cook 20 minutes. Remove pork to separate plate.

• In same skillet saute onions, celery and bell peppers. Add pork, noodles, soup, cream, peas and salt and pepper to taste.

• Spoon into buttered 4-quart (4 L) baking dish and sprinkle with breadcrumbs and walnuts. Bake 30 minutes or until casserole bubbles around edges.

●　　●　　●

• • • • • • • • • • •

Apple Pork Chops

4 butter-flied pork chops
2 apples, peeled, cored
2 teaspoons butter   10 ml
2 tablespoons brown sugar   30 ml

• Place pork chops in non-stick sprayed shallow baking
  dish. Season with salt and pepper.

• Cover and bake at 350° (176° C) for 30 minutes.
  Uncover and place apple halves on top of pork chops.

• Add a little butter and a little brown sugar on each
  apple. Bake for another 15 minutes.

Peach-Pineapple
Baked Ham

1 (3 - 4) pound boneless smoked ham   1.3 kg
4 tablespoons dijon-style mustard, divided   60 ml
1 cup peach preserves   240 ml
1 cup pineapple preserves   240 ml

• Preheat oven to 325° (162° C). Spread 2 tablespoons
  (30 ml) mustard on ham.

• Place ham in prepared, shallow baking pan and bake
  for 20 minutes.

• Combine remaining 2 tablespoons (30 ml) mustard
  and both preserves and heat in microwave oven for
  20 seconds (or in small saucepan at low heat for
  2 to 3 minutes). Pour over ham and bake for about
  15 minutes.

• • • • • • • • • • •

Pork Picante

1 pound pork tenderloin, cubed	.5 kg
2 tablespoons taco seasoning	30 ml
1 cup chunky salsa	240 ml
⅓ cup peach preserves	80 ml

• Toss pork with taco seasoning and brown with a little oil in skillet. Stir in salsa and preserves. Bring to boil. Lower heat and simmer 30 minutes. Pour over hot cooked rice.

• • •

Italian Sausage and Ravioli

1 pound sweet Italian pork sausage, casing removed	.5 kg
1 (1 pound, 10 ounce) jar extra chunky mushroom and green pepper spaghetti sauce	.5 kg/280 g
1 (24 ounce) package frozen cheese-filled ravioli, cooked, drained	680 g
Grated parmesan cheese	

• In roasting pan over medium heat, cook sausage according to package directions or until brown and no longer pink and stir to separate meat.

• Stir in spaghetti sauce. Heat to boiling. Add ravioli and heat through, stirring occasionally.

• Pour into serving dish and sprinkle with parmesan cheese.

Seafood Specials

• • • • • • • • • •

Speedy Jambalaya

¼ pound bacon	114 g
1 pound fresh okra, sliced	.5 kg
2 onions, chopped	
2 (15 ounce) cans stewed tomatoes	2 (425 g)
1 (15 ounce) can whole kernel corn	425 g
1 (16 ounce) package frozen salad shrimp, thawed	.5 kg
1 (6 ounce) box long grain and wild rice	168 g

• In large skillet, fry bacon until crisp. Remove bacon with slotted spoon, leaving bacon drippings in skillet. Crumble bacon and set aside.

• In same skillet, saute okra and onion, but do not brown. Add tomatoes and corn. Bring to boil, reduce heat to medium and simmer about 10 minutes or until most liquid absorbs. Stir in well-drained shrimp and heat just until mixture is thoroughly hot.

• Cook rice according to package directions and serve Jambalaya over rice. Sprinkle crumbled bacon over top of Jambalaya.

● ● ●

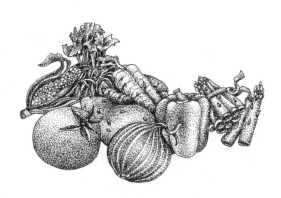

• • • • • • • • • •

Gulf Coast Casserole

2 (10 ounce) cans cream of chicken soup	2 (280 g)
²/₃ cup mayonnaise	160 ml
¹/₃ cup milk	80 ml
3 ribs celery, sliced	
2 tablespoons white wine Worcestershire sauce	30 ml
1 (16 ounce) package frozen salad shrimp, thawed	.5 kg
1 (6 ounce) can crabmeat, drained	168 g
2 tablespoons dried parsley flakes	30 ml
Hot, buttered rice	

• Preheat oven to 350° (176° C). In large bowl, combine soup, mayonnaise, milk, celery and Worcestershire and mix well. Stir in well-drained shrimp, crabmeat and parsley.

• Spoon into greased 3-quart (3 L) baking dish, cover and bake for 45 minutes. Serve with hot, buttered white rice.

● ● ●

Boiled Shrimp

3 pounds fresh shrimp	1.3 kg
2 teaspoons seafood seasoning	10 ml
½ cup vinegar	120 ml

• Remove heads from shrimp. Place shrimp, 1 teaspoon (5 ml) salt, seasoning and vinegar in large saucepan. Cover shrimp with water and bring to a boil. Reduce heat and boil for 10 minutes. Remove from heat, drain and chill in refrigerator.

Angel Hair and Crab Bake

1 onion, chopped	
1 bell pepper, chopped	
2 ribs celery, chopped	
6 tablespoons (¾ stick) butter	90 ml
1 teaspoon dried basil	5 ml
1 teaspoon parsley flakes	5 ml
2 (15 ounce) cans Italian stewed tomatoes	2 (425 g)
½ cup dry white wine	120 ml
1 pound crabmeat, picked, flaked	.5 kg
1 (10 ounce) package angel hair pasta, cooked	280 g
⅓ cup parmesan cheese	80 ml

- In large saucepan, saute onion, bell pepper and celery in melted butter. Stir in basil, parsley flakes and salt and pepper to taste.

- Add stewed tomatoes and wine. Bring to boil, reduce heat and simmer 5 minutes.

- Add crabmeat and simmer 10 minutes. Spread angel hair pasta on serving platter and top with crab-mixture. Sprinkle parmesan over crab-mixture.

• • • • • • • • • •

Florentine Shrimp and Pasta

2 (9 ounce) frozen boil-in-bag creamed spinach	2 (255 g)
1 (12 ounce) package penne pasta	340 g
¼ cup heavy cream	60 ml
1 teaspoon Cajun seasoning	5 ml
2 tablespoons olive oil	30 ml
1 pound peeled, medium shrimp	.5 kg

• Bring large pot of water to boil and add spinach pouches. Cook according to package directions.

• In another large saucepan, cook pasta according to package directions. Drain, add cream and Cajun seasoning and mix until they blend.

• In skillet with olive oil, cook shrimp about 3 minutes or until thoroughly cooked (but not over-cooked.)

• Cut spinach pouches and add to pasta. Stir in shrimp and transfer to serving dish.

●   ●   ●

Garlic Shrimp-Couscous

24 fresh or frozen large shrimp, thawed	
1 tablespoon olive oil	15 ml
3 teaspoons minced garlic	15 ml
1 teaspoon dried, crushed tarragon	5 ml
1 (5.6 ounce) package toasted pine nut	
couscous mix	155 g
1¼ cups chicken broth	300 ml
1 (8 ounce) jar roasted red bell peppers	227 g
3 fresh green onions, sliced	
⅓ cup fresh lemon juice	80 ml
¼ cup (½ stick) butter, melted	60 ml

• Peel, vein shrimp and pat dry. Place shrimp in sealable plastic bag and add oil, garlic and tarragon. Seal bag and turn to coat shrimp. Marinate in refrigerator for 1 hour.

• Prepare couscous according to package directions but use 1¼ cups (300 ml) chicken broth. Stir in bell peppers and onions and set aside.

• In small bowl, combine lemon juice and butter. In large skillet, cook and stir shrimp with marinade over medium heat for 4 minutes or until shrimp turn opaque. Drain and drizzle lemon-butter mixture over shrimp.

● ● ●

• • • • • • • • • •

Crispy Flounder

⅓ cup mayonnaise	80 ml
1 pound flounder fillets	.5 kg
1 cup seasoned breadcrumbs	240 ml
¼ cup grated parmesan cheese	60 ml

• Place mayonnaise in small dish. Coat fish with mayonnaise and dip in crumbs to coat well.

• Arrange in shallow baking dish. Bake uncovered at 375° (190° C) for 25 minutes.

• • •

Flounder Au Gratin

½ cup fine dry breadcrumbs	120 ml
¼ cup grated parmesan cheese	60 ml
1 pound flounder	.5 kg
⅓ cup mayonnaise	80 ml

• In shallow dish, combine crumbs and cheese.

• Brush both sides of fish with mayonnaise and coat with crumb mixture.

• Arrange filets in single layer in shallow pan and bake at 375° (190° C) for 20 to 25 minutes or until fish flakes easily.

• • •

• • • • • • • • • • •

Orange Roughy with Peppers

1 pound orange roughy filets	.5 kg
1 onion, sliced	
2 red bell peppers, cut into julienne strips	
1 teaspoon dried thyme leaves	5 ml

• Cut fish into 4 serving-size pieces.

• Heat a little oil in skillet, layer onion and bell peppers in oil and sprinkle with half thyme and ⅛ teaspoon (.5 ml) pepper.

• Place fish over peppers and sprinkle with remaining thyme and pepper.

• Turn burner on high just until fish begins to cook.

• Lower heat, cover and cook fish for 15 to 20 minutes or until fish flakes easily.

Chipper Fish

2 pounds sole or orange roughy	1 kg
½ cup Caesar salad dressing	120 ml
1 cup crushed potato chips	240 ml
½ cup shredded cheddar cheese	120 ml

• Dip fish in dressing and place in greased baking dish.

• Combine potato chips and cheese and sprinkle over fish.

• Bake at 375° (190° C) for about 20 to 25 minutes.

Desserts
So Sweet

Cherry-Pecan Pie

1 (14 ounce) can sweetened condensed milk	396 g
¼ cup lemon juice	60 ml
1 (8 ounce) carton whipped topping	227 g
1 cup chopped pecans	240 ml
1 (20 ounce) can cherry pie filling	567 g
2 (9-inch) graham cracker piecrusts	2 (23 cm)

- Combine condensed milk and lemon juice, stir well and fold in whipped topping.

- Fold pecans and pie filling into mixture. Spoon into piecrusts. Chill overnight.

Thanksgiving Pie

1 (15 ounce) can pumpkin	425 g
1 cup sugar	240 ml
2 eggs, beaten	
1½ teaspoons pumpkin pie spice	7 ml
1 (12 ounce) can evaporated milk	340 g
1 (9-inch) piecrust, unbaked	23 cm

- Preheat oven to 425° (220° C).

- In bowl, combine pumpkin, sugar, eggs, pumpkin pie spice, evaporated milk and a dash of salt and mix well. Pour mixture into piecrust and bake 15 minutes.

- Lower heat to 325° (162° C) and continue baking another 50 minutes or until knife inserted in center of pie comes out clean.

• • • • • • • • • •

Million Dollar Pie

24 round, buttery crackers, crumbled
1 cup chopped pecans 240 ml
4 egg whites (absolutely no yolks at all)
1 cup sugar 240 ml

• Preheat oven to 350° (176° C). In bowl, combine cracker crumbs with pecans.

• In separate mixing bowl, beat egg whites until stiff and slowly add sugar while still mixing.

• Gently fold crumbs and pecan mixture into egg whites and pour into pie pan. Bake for 20 minutes and cool before serving.

• • •

Chocolate-Cream Cheese Pie

1 (8 ounce) package cream cheese, softened 227 g
¾ cup powdered sugar 180 ml
¼ cup cocoa 60 ml
1 (8 ounce) container whipped topping, thawed 227 g
1 (9-inch) prepared crumb piecrust 23 cm
½ cup chopped pecans 120 ml

• Combine cream cheese, sugar and cocoa in mixing bowl and beat at medium speed until creamy.

• Add whipped topping and fold until smooth. Spread in piecrust, sprinkle pecans over top and refrigerate.

• • • • • • • • • •

Chocolate-Coconut Pie

1½ cups flaked coconut	360 ml
1½ cups chopped pecans	360 ml
1 (12 ounce) package chocolate chips	340 g
1 (6 ounce) prepared graham cracker piecrust	168 g
1 (14 ounce) can sweetened condensed milk	396 g

• Preheat oven to 350° (176° C).

• Combine coconut, pecans and chocolate chips. Sprinkle mixture over piecrust.

• Spoon sweetened condensed milk evenly over coconut mixture.

• Bake for 25 to 30 minutes. Cool before serving.

● ● ●

Cherry Crisp

2 (20 ounce) cans cherry pie filling	2 (567g)
1 (18 ounce) box white cake mix	510 g
½ cup (1 stick) butter	120 ml
2 cups chopped pecans	480 ml

• Pour pie filling into greased 9 x 13-inch (23 x 33 cm) baking dish.

• Sprinkle cake mix over top of filling.

• Dot with butter and cover with pecans.

• Bake uncovered at 350° (176° C) for 45 minutes.

• • • • • • • • • • •

Strawberry Pound Cake

1 (18 ounce) box strawberry cake mix	510 g
1 (3.4 ounce) package instant pineapple pudding mix	100 g
1/3 cup oil	80 ml
4 eggs	
1 (3 ounce) package strawberry gelatin	84 g

• Preheat oven to 350° (176° C).

• Mix all ingredients plus 1 cup (240 ml) water and beat for 2 minutes at medium speed.

• Pour into greased, floured bundt pan.

• Bake for 55 to 60 minutes. Cake is done when toothpick inserted in center comes out clean.

• Cool for 20 minutes before removing cake from pan. If you would like an icing, use commercial vanilla icing.

Tip: If you like coconut better than pineapple, use coconut cream pudding mix.

● 　 ● 　 ●

• • • • • • • • • • •

Cherry-Nut Cake

1 (18 ounce) box French vanilla cake mix	510 g
½ cup (1 stick) butter, melted	120 ml
2 eggs	
1 (20 ounce) can cherry pie filling	567 g
1 cup chopped pecans	240 ml

• In large bowl, mix all ingredients by hand.

• Pour into greased, floured bundt or tube pan.

• Bake at 350° (176° C) for 1 hour. (Sprinkle some powdered sugar on top of cake if you would like a sweeter cake.)

●   ●   ●

Hawaiian-Pineapple Cake

1 (20 ounce) can crushed pineapple, drained	567 g
1 (20 ounce) can cherry pie filling	567 g
1 (18 ounce) box yellow cake mix	510 g
1 cup (2 sticks) butter, softened	240 ml
1¼ cups chopped pecans	300 ml

• Place all ingredients in large bowl and mix by hand.

• Pour into greased, floured 9 x 13-inch (23 x 33 cm) baking dish.

• Bake at 350° (176° C) for 1 hour 10 minutes.

●   ●   ●

Lemon-Poppy Seed Cake

1 (18 ounce) box lemon cake mix with pudding	510 g
1 (8 ounce) carton sour cream	227 g
3 eggs	
⅓ cup oil	80 ml
⅓ cup poppy seeds	80 ml

- Preheat oven to 350° (176° C).

- Prepare 12-cup (3 L) bundt pan with non-stick spray. (Use spray that already contains flour.)

- In mixing bowl, combine dry cake mix, sour cream, eggs, oil and ¼ cup (60 ml) water and beat on medium speed until ingredients mix well.

- Stir in poppy seeds and mix until seeds are evenly distributed. Pour batter into prepared bundt pan.

- Bake for 45 minutes and test for doneness with toothpick. Cool.

    Tip: If you like, you can dust cake with powdered sugar or spread prepared vanilla icing on top of cake.

Deluxe Coconut Cake

1 (18 ounce) package yellow cake mix	510 g
1 (14 ounce) can sweetened condensed milk	396 g
1 (10 ounce) can coconut cream	280 g
1 (4 ounce) can flaked coconut	114 g
1 (8 ounce) carton whipped topping	227 g

• Prepare cake batter according to package directions and pour into greased, floured 9 x 13-inch (23 x 33 cm) baking pan.

• Bake at 350° (176° C) for 30 to 35 minutes or until toothpick inserted in center comes out clean.

• While cake is warm, punch holes in cake about 2 inches (5 cm) apart.

• Pour sweetened condensed milk over cake and spread around until all milk soaks into cake.

• Pour coconut cream over cake and sprinkle coconut over top.

• When cake is cool, frost with whipped topping. Chill before serving.

• • • • • • • • • • •

Old-Fashioned Applesauce Cake

1 (18 ounce) box spice cake mix	510 g
3 eggs	
1¼ cups applesauce	300 ml
⅓ cup oil	80 ml
1 cup chopped pecans	240 ml

• With mixer, combine dry cake mix, eggs, applesauce and oil. Beat at medium speed for 2 minutes. Stir in pecans.

• Pour into greased, floured 9 x 13-inch (23 x 33 cm) baking pan.

• Bake at 350° (176° C) for 40 minutes. Test for doneness with toothpick and cool.

• For frosting, use prepared vanilla frosting and stir in ½ teaspoon (2 ml) cinnamon before spreading on cake.

● ● ●

• • • • • • • • • •

Chess Cake

1 (18 ounce) box yellow cake mix	510 g
2 eggs	
½ cup (1 stick) butter, softened	120 ml

• Beat cake mix, eggs and butter. Press into greased
  9 x 13-inch (23 x 33 cm) baking pan.

Topping:

2 eggs	
1 (8 ounce) package cream cheese, softened	227 g
1 (16 ounce) box powdered sugar	.5 kg

• Beat 2 eggs, cream cheese and powdered sugar. Pour
  topping mixture over cake batter. Bake at 350°
  (176° C) for 35 minutes.

• • •

Easy Sand Tarts

1 cup (2 sticks) butter, softened	240 ml
¾ cup powdered sugar	180 ml
2 cups sifted flour	480 ml
1 cup chopped pecans	240 ml
1 teaspoon vanilla extract	5 ml

• Preheat oven to 325° (162° C). In mixing bowl, cream
  butter and powdered sugar. Slowly add flour, pecans
  and vanilla.

• Form into balls and place on ungreased baking sheet.
  Bake for 20 minutes. Roll in extra powdered sugar
  after tarts cool.

• • • • • • • • • •

Snappy Almond-Sugar Cookies

1 cup (2 sticks) butter, softened	240 ml
1 cup plus 2 tablespoons sugar, divided	240 ml/
	30 ml
½ teaspoon almond extract	2 ml
2 cups flour	480 ml
1 cup chopped almonds	240 ml

• Cream butter, 1 cup (240 ml) sugar and almond extract until light and fluffy. Slowly beat in flour and stir in almonds.

• Shape dough into roll, wrap and chill well, about 2 hours.

• Preheat oven to 325° (162° C).

• Slice roll into ¼-inch (.6 cm) pieces and bake for 20 minutes.

• Sprinkle with remaining 2 tablespoons (30 ml) sugar while still hot.

● ● ●

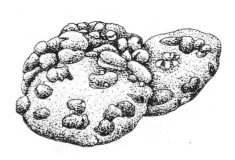

Double-Chocolate Cookies

6 egg whites	
3 cups powdered sugar	360 g
¼ cup cocoa	20 g
3½ cups finely chopped pecans	390 g

- Beat egg whites until light and frothy. Fold sugar and cocoa into egg whites and beat lightly. Fold in pecans.

- Drop by teaspoons on lightly greased, floured cookie sheet.

- Bake at 325º (160° C) for about 20 minutes. Do not over bake and cool completely before removing from cookie sheet.

Coconut Macaroons

2 (7 ounce) packages flaked coconut	2 (200 g)
1 (14 ounce) can sweetened condensed milk	395 g
2 teaspoons vanilla	10 ml
½ teaspoon almond extract	2 ml

- In mixing bowl, combine coconut, condensed milk and extracts and mix well.

- Drop by rounded teaspoons onto foil-lined cookie sheet.

- Bake at 350º (176° C) for 8 to 10 minutes or until light brown around edges. Immediately remove from foil. (Macaroons will stick if allowed to cool.) Store at room temperature.

• • • • • • • • • • •

Lemon Cookies

½ cup (1 stick) butter, softened	115 g
1⅔ cup sugar	350 g
2 tablespoons lemon juice	30 ml
2 cups flour	240 g

• Cream butter, sugar and lemon juice and slowly stir in flour.

• Drop by teaspoons onto ungreased cookie sheet.

• Bake at 350° (175° C) for 14 to 15 minutes.

• • •

Gingerbread Cookies

¾ cup (1½ sticks) butter, softened	60 g
2 egg yolks	
1 (18 ounce) spice cake mix	510 g
1 teaspoon ginger	5 ml

• In large bowl combine butter and egg yolks. Gradually blend in cake mix and ginger and mix well.

• Roll out to ⅛-inch (.3 cm) thickness on lightly floured surface. Use gingerbread cookie cutter to cut out cookies and place 2 inches (5 cm) apart on cookie sheet.

• Bake at 375° (190° C) for about 8 minutes or until edges are slightly brown. Cool cookies before transferring to cookie bowl.

Disappearing Cookies

1 (18 ounce) box butter cake mix	510 g
1 (3.4 ounce) package butterscotch instant pudding mix	100 g
1 cup oil	240 ml
1 egg, beaten	
1¼ cups chopped pecans	300 ml

- By hand, stir together cake mix and pudding mix and slowly add oil. Add egg and mix thoroughly. Stir in pecans.

- Drop cookie dough by teaspoonfuls about 2 inches (5 cm) apart on baking sheet.

- Bake at 350° (176° C) for 8 or 9 minutes. (Do not overcook.)

Potato Chip Crunchies

1 cup (2 sticks) butter, softened	240 ml
²/₃ cup sugar	160 ml
1 teaspoon vanilla extract	5 ml
1½ cups flour	360 ml
½ cup crushed potato chips	120 ml

- Cream butter, sugar and vanilla and stir in flour. Carefully fold in potato chips. Drop by teaspoonfuls on ungreased baking sheet.

- Bake at 350° (176° C) for about 12 minutes or until light brown.

Butterscotch Cookies

1 (12 ounce) and 1 (6 ounce) package butterscotch chips	340 g/168 g
2¼ cups chow mein noodles	540 ml
½ cup chopped walnuts	120 ml
¼ cup flaked coconut	60 ml

• Melt butterscotch chips in double boiler. Add noodles, walnuts and coconut.

• Drop by tablespoonfuls onto waxed paper.

● ● ●

Scotch Shortbread

½ cup (1 stick) unsalted butter, softened	120 ml
⅓ cup sugar	80 ml
1¼ cups flour	300 ml
Powdered sugar	

• Cream butter and sugar until light and fluffy. Add flour and pinch of salt and mix well.

• Spread dough in 8-inch (20 cm) square pan. Bake at 325° (162° C) for 20 minutes or until light brown.

• Cool shortbread in pan, dust with powdered sugar and cut into squares.

● ● ●

• • • • • • • • • •

Walnut Bars

1²⁄₃ cups graham cracker crumbs	400 ml
1½ cups coarsely chopped walnuts	360 ml
1 (14 ounce) can sweetened condensed milk	396 g
¼ cup coconut (optional)	60 ml

• Place cracker crumbs and walnuts in bowl. Slowly add condensed milk, coconut and a pinch of salt. (Mixture will be very thick.)

• Pack mixture into greased 9-inch (23 cm) square pan with back of spoon. Bake at 350° (176° C) for 35 minutes. When cool, cut into squares.

● ● ●

Rocky Road Bars

1 (12 ounce) package semi-sweet chocolate morsels	340 g
1 (14 ounce) can sweetened condensed milk	396 g
2 tablespoons (¼ stick) butter	30 ml
2 cups dry-roasted peanuts	240 ml
1 (10 ounce) package miniature marshmallows	280 g

• Place chocolate morsels, milk and butter in double boiler and heat on low. Stir constantly until chocolate melts.

• Remove from heat and stir in peanuts and marshmallows.

• Spread mixture quickly onto wax paper-lined 9 x 13-inch (23 x 33 cm) pan. Chill at least 2 hours. Cut into bars and store in refrigerator.

Creamy Pecan Squares

1 (18 ounce) box yellow cake mix	510 g
3 eggs, divided	
½ cup (1 stick) butter, softened	120 ml
2 cups chopped pecans	240 ml
1 (8 ounce) package cream cheese, softened	227 g
3⅔ cups powdered sugar	870 ml

• In mixing bowl, combine cake mix, 1 egg and butter. Stir in pecans and mix well.

• Press into greased 9 x 13-inch (23 x 33 cm) baking pan.

• In mixing bowl, beat cream cheese, sugar and remaining eggs until smooth. Pour over pecan mixture.

• Bake at 350° (176° C) for 55 minutes or until golden brown. Cool and cut into squares.

Toffee Bars

1½ cups (3 sticks) butter, softened	360 ml
1¾ cups packed light brown sugar	420 ml
2 teaspoons vanilla extract	10 ml
3 cups flour	710 ml
1 (8 ounce) package chocolate chips	227 g

• Preheat oven to 350° (176° C).

• In mixing bowl, combine butter, brown sugar and vanilla and beat on medium speed for 3 minutes.

• Add flour, mix until it blends completely and stir in chocolate chips.

• Place dough on greased 9 x 13-inch (23 x 33 cm) baking pan.

• Bake 25 minutes or until light brown. Cool slightly and cut into bars.

• • • • • • • • • • •

Snicker Brownies

1 (18 ounce) German chocolate cake mix	510 g
¾ cup (1½ sticks) butter, melted	180 ml
½ cup evaporated milk	120 ml
4 (3 ounce) snicker candy bars, cut in	
⅛-inch slices	84 g/.3 cm

• In large bowl, combine cake mix, butter and evaporated milk. Beat on low speed until mixture blends well.

• Add half batter into greased, floured 9 x 13-inch (23 x 33 cm) baking pan. Bake at 350° (176° C) for 10 minutes.

• Remove from oven and place candy bar slices evenly over brownies. Drop remaining half of batter by spoonfuls over candy bars and spread as evenly as possible. Place back in oven and bake for 20 minutes longer. When cool, cut into bars.

• • •

Nutty Blonde Brownies

1 (1 pound) box light brown sugar	.5 kg
4 eggs	
2 cups biscuit mix	480 ml
2 cups chopped pecans	480 ml

• In mixing bowl, beat brown sugar, eggs and biscuit mix. Stir in pecans and pour into greased 9 x 13-inch (23 x 33 cm) baking pan. Bake at 350° (176° C) for 35 minutes. Cool and cut into squares.

No-Cook Lemon Balls

2 cups graham cracker crumbs, almond or pecan shortbread cookie crumbs, divided	480 ml
1 (6 ounce) can frozen lemonade concentrate, thawed	168 g
½ cup (1 stick) butter, softened	120 ml
1 (16 ounce) box powdered sugar, sifted	.5 kg

• Combine 1½ cups (360 ml) cookie crumbs, lemonade concentrate, butter and powdered sugar. Shape into small balls.

• Roll in reserved cookie crumbs and put on wax paper.

• Refrigerate 3 to 4 hours in sealed container or freeze to serve later.

Apricot Bars

1¼ cups flour	300 ml
¾ cup packed brown sugar	180 ml
6 tablespoons (¾ stick) butter	90 ml
¾ cup apricot preserves	180 ml

• In mixing bowl, combine flour, brown sugar and butter and mix well.

• Place half mixture in 9-inch (23 cm) square baking pan. Spread apricot preserves over top of mixture. Add remaining flour mixture over top of dessert.

• Bake at 350° (176° C) for 30 minutes. Cut into bars.

• • • • • • • • • • •

Porcupine Clusters

¼ cup corn syrup	60 ml
1 (12 ounce) package white chocolate morsels	340 g
2 cups chow mein noodles	480 ml
¾ cup salted peanuts	180 ml

• On low heat, melt corn syrup and white chocolate chips. Pour over noodles and peanuts and mix well.

• Drop by teaspoonfuls on waxed paper.

• Refrigerate to harden. Store in airtight container.

● ● ●

Butterscotch Crunchies

1 (12 ounce) package of butterscotch morsels	340 g
1¾ cups chow mein noodles	420 ml
1 cup chopped pecans	240 ml

• Melt butterscotch morsels in heavy pan over very low flame and stir gently.

• Stir in noodles and pecans just until they blend and are coat with butterscotch.

• Drop mixture by teaspoonful onto waxed paper. Refrigerate 30 minutes or until set.

● ● ●

• • • • • • • • • •

Butterscotch Surprise

1 (12 ounce) package butterscotch morsels	340 g
2 cups chow mein noodles	480 ml
1 cup dry roasted peanuts	240 ml

• In saucepan, heat butterscotch morsels over low heat until they melt completely. Add noodles and peanuts and stir until each piece is coated with butterscotch.

• Drop from spoon onto waxed paper. Cool and store in airtight container.

● ● ●

Kids' Bars

1 cup sugar	240 ml
1 cup light corn syrup	240 ml
1½ cups crunchy peanut butter	360 ml
6 cups crispy rice cereal	1.5 L
1 (12 ounce) package chocolate chips	340 g

• In saucepan, combine sugar and corn syrup. Bring to a boil, stirring constantly. Remove from heat and stir in peanut butter and crispy rice cereal.

• Spread into buttered 9 x 13-inch (23 x 33 cm) pan.

• In saucepan over low heat, melt chocolate chips. Spread over cereal layer. Refrigerate until set and cut into bars. Store in refrigerator.

● ● ●

• • • • • • • • • •

Hazel's Nutty Fudge

1 (12 ounce) package white chocolate chips	340 g
¾ cup hazelnut-cocoa spread	180 ml
1½ cups chopped hazelnuts, divided	360 ml

• In medium saucepan over low heat, melt white chocolate chips and add hazelnut spread. Cook and stir until mixture blends well.

• Remove from heat and stir in 1 cup (240 ml) hazelnuts. Drop by teaspoons on waxed paper. Garnish with reserved hazelnuts. Refrigerate until set.

● ● ●

Macadamia Candy

2 (3 ounce) jars macadamia nuts	2 (84 g)
1 (20 ounce) package white almond bark	567 g
¾ cup flaked coconut	180 ml

• Heat dry skillet and toast nuts until slightly golden. (Some brands of macadamia nuts are already toasted.) Set aside.

• In double boiler, melt 12 squares almond bark. As soon as almond bark melts, pour in macadamia nuts and coconut and stir well.

• Place wax paper on cookie sheet, pour candy on waxed paper and spread out. Refrigerate 30 minutes to set. Break into pieces.

● ● ●

• • • • • • • • • • •

A

B

C

• • • • • • • • • • •

● ● ● ● ● ● ● ● ● ● ●

● ● ● ● ● ● ● ● ● ●

• • • • • • • • • • •

COOKBOOKS PUBLISHED BY COOKBOOK RESOURCES, LLC

The Ultimate Cooking with 4 Ingredients
Easy Cooking with 5 Ingredients
The Best of Cooking with 3 Ingredients
Gourmet Cooking with 5 Ingredients
Healthy Cooking with 4 Ingredients
Diabetic Cooking with 4 Ingredients
4-Ingredient Recipes for 30-Minute Meals
Essential 3-4-5 Ingredient Recipes
The Best 1001 Short, Easy Recipes
Easy Slow-Cooker Cookbook
Essential Slow-Cooker Cooking
Quick Fixes with Cake Mixes
Casseroles to the Rescue
I Ain't On No Diet Cookbook
Kitchen Keepsakes/More Kitchen Keepsakes
Old-Fashioned Cookies
Grandmother's Cookies
Mother's Recipes
Recipe Keepsakes
Cookie Dough Secrets
Gifts for the Cookie Jar
All New Gifts for the Cookie Jar
Gifts in a Pickle Jar
Muffins In A Jar
Brownies In A Jar
Cookie Jar Magic
Easy Desserts
Bake Sale Bestsellers
Quilters' Cooking Companion
Miss Sadie's Southern Cooking
Classic Tex-Mex and Texas Cooking
Classic Southwest Cooking
The Great Canadian Cookbook
The Best of Lone Star Legacy Cookbook
Cookbook 25 Years
Pass the Plate
Texas Longhorn Cookbook
Trophy Hunters' Wild Game Cookbook
Mealtimes and Memories
Holiday Recipes
Little Taste of Texas
Little Taste of Texas II
Texas Peppers
Southwest Sizzler
Southwest Olé
Class Treats
Leaving Home
Easy One-Dish Meals
Easy Casseroles

To Order: **Easy Potluck Recipes**

Please send_____ paperback copies @ $12.95 (U.S.) each $ _____

Texas residents add sales tax @ $1.06 each $ _____

Plus postage/handling @ $6.00 (1st copy) $ _____

$1.00 (each additional copy) $ _____

Check or Credit Card (Canada-credit card only) Total $ _____

Charge to: ❑ MasterCard or ❑ VISA

Account # _____

Expiration Date _____

Signature_____

Name _____

Address_____

City_____State_____Zip_____

Telephone (day_____(Evening)_____

Mail or Call:
Cookbook Resources
541 Doubletree Dr.
Highland Village, Texas 75077
Toll Free (866) 229-2665
(972) 317-6404 Fax

To Order: **Easy Potluck Recipes**

Please send_____ paperback copies @ $12.95 (U.S.) each $ _____

Texas residents add sales tax @ $1.06 each $ _____

Plus postage/handling @ $6.00 (1st copy) $ _____

$1.00 (each additional copy) $ _____

Check or Credit Card (Canada-credit card only) Total $ _____

Charge to: ❑ MasterCard or ❑ VISA

Account # _____

Expiration Date _____

Signature_____

Name _____

Address_____

City_____State_____Zip_____

Telephone (Day)_____(Evening)_____

Mail or Call:
Cookbook Resources
541 Doubletree Dr.
Highland Village, Texas 75077
Toll Free (866) 229-2665
(972) 317-6404 Fax